ONE HAND CLAPPING
A Memoir of Childhood

BY THE SAME AUTHOR:

THE GOLDEN VALLEY
RECOLLECTIONS OF A GHOST
A PATH TO THE SEA
PRIVATE VIEW

as 'Richard Cowper':

BREAKTHROUGH
PHOENIX
DOMINO
KULDESAK
CLONE
TIME OUT OF MIND
THE TWILIGHT OF BRIAREUS
WORLDS APART

ONE HAND CLAPPING

A Memoir of Childhood

by

COLIN MIDDLETON MURRY

LONDON
VICTOR GOLLANCZ LTD
1975

ISBN 0 575 01901 8

PRINTED IN GREAT BRITAIN
BY EBENEZER BAYLIS AND SON LTD
THE TRINITY PRESS, WORCESTER, AND LONDON

For my sisters

with love

'. . . another John Middleton, ye gods!'

D. H. Lawrence on learning of my birth

LIST OF ILLUSTRATIONS

ONE HAND CLAPPING

I

I ONCE read somewhere that the age at which a child usually becomes aware of its identity—of being 'me'—is around seven or eight. If that is true then in this as in so many other ways I must be accounted a late starter, for I remember most clearly the moment at which I first came to believe in my own unique and separate existence.

I was, I suppose, about twelve years old and was indulging my immoderate appetite for probing into the private lives and secrets of those around me. In those days few things escaped my far from innocent eye. Bundles of faded letters in forgotten trunks; the stub ends of old cheque books; mysterious pieces of medical equipment stored carefully out of reach in the backs of bathroom cupboards; the contents of ladies' handbags; any locked drawer; anything handwritten; anything, in short, that I could believe I was not meant to see. I was never quite sure what I was hoping to find but, even so, I recognized it when I *did* find it. It was a clue, the only one I was ever to stumble across, to the mystery of my own existence.

The form it took was that of a grey, page-a-day, desk diary for the year 1925 which had somehow become lodged behind the back of one of the drawers in an otherwise empty bureau in the spare bedroom of the Norfolk rectory where I spent much of my childhood. As I eased the drawer open my sharp ears caught the sound of something slipping down at the back. In a second I had the drawer out and was groping within the dusty cavity. My questing fingertips touched and drew out this treasure. I turned over the yellowing pages and at once recognized my father's handwriting. Carefully I replaced the drawer; slid the slender, cardboard covered book up inside my jumper; strolled nonchalantly along the landing and ducked down into one of my secret hideouts in the inner box-room.

Having clambered to the top of a stack of mattresses by way of a broken harmonium I stretched out on my stomach, propped my head in my hands and began to read.

I soon realized that my father was not much better at keeping up a diary than I was myself. There were a few scattered references to my sister Katherine—ever afterwards known by her nickname of 'Weg'—who was born in the April of that year, and one or two to other people whose names I recognized—H. M. Tomlinson, Jimmy Young, my father's brother Richard. I turned the pages, many of them blank, and then suddenly my eye was caught by an entry which was far from being of the 'de la Mares to tea' type. In it he described how my mother had called him into the bathroom one evening, ostensibly to help her read the bathroom scales. What had followed was very human and had obviously been very much enjoyed by them both. I certainly enjoyed reading about it. At the end of the page my father had added a postscript to the effect that he prayed Violet would not conceive again so soon after my sister's birth.

I flipped on rapidly through the sprinkle of entries for the rest of that month and half way through those for September I found what I was looking for. My mother had announced to him that she was pregnant again. One bleak sentence in his account of it stood out from all the rest. 'She wept as though her heart was broken and there was nothing I could say that would comfort her.'

I lifted my head and gazed out of the cobwebby window to where the nesting swallows swooped and flickered against the high eaves of the house. Gradually a sort of smothering misery enveloped me. A slow, hot tear plopped off the end of my nose and splashed plumb in the middle of that sad entry. I don't suppose I had ever felt lonelier in my life, and yet, for the first time in that life I was aware that my mother really *had* existed: by those tears she had shed she had become imaginatively real to me. And it was at that precise moment that I became aware of my 'self'—or, rather, I became aware of *a* self that had its lodging within my body and now peered out at the world through the bleared windows that were my eyes. I think I realized then that nothing could ever be quite the same again, though I would have been hard put to it to explain precisely how things had changed. Even now I am not sure. So what follows must be seen as a belated attempt to come to terms with that experience; to see myself as I was then and, perhaps, through doing so, to discover what I have since become.

2

I WAS born in the Old Coastguard Station, Abbotsbury, Dorset, on May 9th, 1926, the day the General Strike was declared. When, years later, I discovered this coincidence it seemed to me singularly appropriate, as though the whole country had thrown up its hands in protest and cried: 'Oh no! this is *too* much!'

For some reason which was never explained to me but which I now suspect may well have been simple absent-mindedness on my father's part, I was registered in precisely the same names as himself. My nickname 'Colin'—immediately shortened to 'Col'—was apparently wished upon me by my father's mother.

At the time of my birth Violet, my mother, was twenty-five years old and looked nineteen; my father, John Middleton Murry, was thirty-eight and looked over forty. He was then arguably at the peak of his fame as a critic and editor; she was just beginning to emerge, like an imago from its chrysalis, as a writer of short stories and sketches in the Mansfield/Chekhov tradition. But the gulf which separated them was more than just a matter of years. Their love for each other—which was real enough—was founded upon an illusion, for my father unwittingly chose to see in Violet the heaven-sent reincarnation of his first wife Katherine Mansfield who had died in 1923.

Aided by an uncanny physical resemblance to Katherine, Violet strove to live up to the fiction. So successful was she that it seems to have taken my father the better part of three years to discover that she was not, in fact, Katherine. By then it was already too late. Totally identified with her rôle, Violet contracted Katherine's disease. When my father heard the dreaded sentence he "went down into the depths". But worse was to come. When he told her the specialist's verdict on the bacteriological analysis—that she had pulmonary tuberculosis—her reaction was, to him, totally incomprehensible. In his journal he describes it thus:

"'Oh I'm so *glad*!' she cried, 'I wanted this to happen.'

I stared into her shining eyes. 'You wanted this to happen,' I repeated, slowly and dully, while my world turned upside down.

'You see, Golly,' she explained, 'I wanted you to love me as much as you loved Katherine—and how could you, without this?'"

At the time of this thunderclap I was eight months old. My birth seems to have set the final seal on my mother's fate. Certainly she never recovered from it. I was handed over to a nurse while my father directed all his energies to restoring Violet to health. Perhaps I divined that I was not getting what I considered to be my fair share of love and attention. Obstinately I declined to thrive. In January 1927 I was despatched summarily to hospital with, of all things, suspected T.B.! By the time I was returned and my illness had been pronounced a false alarm, my mother had departed for the Edward VII sanatorium in Midhurst where she was to remain from May until October 1927.

For the better part of forty years I cherished the belief that my mother had died when I was two years old. Only in this way could I explain to myself why I had only one memory of her. Nevertheless, the fact is that I was nearly five when, in March 1931, Violet gave up the struggle to live. According to my father's account the news, when he broke it to my sister and me, appears to have made little impression as far as I was concerned—"Weg thought a little while, and said: 'It's a good thing you didn't die, Dadda. Then we should only have had Maud and Miss Cockbayne.' And Col, as usual going to extremes said: 'If Maud and Miss Cockbayne had died too . . .' 'I expect,' said Weg, 'that we should have found another house to go in.' I don't think (commented my father) it meant anything to Col."

I daresay he was right at that. From my point of view if my mother could be said to have existed at all it was as a negation. Today I can understand her total rejection of me, just as, from the vantage point of hindsight, I can understand my father's extraordinary life-long ambiguity towards me. Somehow I just didn't fit into the pattern of things. Subconsciously he must, at least in part, have blamed me for Violet's illness and death and the ten years of unrelieved misery which followed it.

The immediate effect this two-fold rejection had upon me was to make me inordinately jealous of my sister. She was first in the love queue and I resented it. My only recourse was to take it out on her whenever I got the chance. Strangely enough she seems to have been only too ready to forgive me. Perhaps she felt dimly that I had a case, or maybe she just had a sweet nature, but she stuck up for me loyally and pleaded my cause through her tears. This served to endear her still further to my father who regarded me, with some justification, as at best a changeling.

When, in the autumn of 1927, it became obvious to him that Violet was not responding to the treatment at Midhurst, he resolved to bring her back to the Coastguard Station and nurse her himself. In an unpublished fragment of autobiography he has given the following account of that time:

"It was a queer timeless existence that winter. The Coastguard Station, at any rate in those days, was remote enough in the summer; but in the winter it was isolated indeed. The Atlantic breakers pounded incessantly against the beach at the bottom of the tamarisk garden, and a faint tremor seemed to shake the earth and the long low house continually. But for the rest I remember very little, save the sense that we were totally withdrawn from the world—a tiny little community whose only contact with the life beyond was the postman, a handsome middle-aged man with a splendid white moustache, who battled his way along the coast road every morning. . . ."

The "little community" consisted of himself, Violet, Weg,

me and our nurse, who lived in one pair of the four adjoining cottages which went to make up "the white house by the sea". At the other end lived the Tomlinsons. The fourth cottage was occupied by transient tenants.

It is from this period that I date my first dim memories—of a wilderness of stones that was the Chesil Bank; of a brass hot-water can that 'belonged' to my sister and which I coveted and one day stole. On discovering my crime my sister pursued me, loudly lamenting my enormity, whereupon I slammed the door on her. In so doing I trapped her little finger in the hinge jamb. The memory of that moment is frozen in me for life. A tiny, white, pear-shaped morself of flesh squeezed into the crack of the door and a thin scarlet thread of blood. It was not the first wound I gave Weg nor the last but it is the only one whose visible scar survives to this day.

I suspect that a psychologist would see in that incident an attempt to steal some of the love that I felt should have been mine. If so it was a singularly unsuccessful venture. A line was firmly drawn across the threshold of my mother's bedroom and I was not permitted to cross it. The reason, I have since been told, was that I was regarded as being susceptible to her disease. Naturally I did not understand this. Still less did I understand why my sister was permitted to enter where I was not. Every morning after breakfast my father would gather her up into his arms and retreat with her into the sanctum from which I was excluded. The door was closed and that was that. In the circumstances it does not altogether surprise me that not only have I erased virtually every trace of my mother from my memory but, having since once passed within a mile of the Old Coastguard Station, I felt no pressing curiosity to re-visit it.

By the autumn of that year it had become apparent to my father that the recovery he had worked so hard to bring about was not to be. What he *had* achieved by his devotion was remarkable enough, for in the spring of that year he had been able to write to T. S. Eliot that Violet's condition had "improved immensely since December, when it was zero. It is supposed to be a miracle—certainly it is contrary to all prognosis—that she is now alive". Nevertheless, by September it was obvious that the course of the disease, though slowed, had not been arrested. To stay on in Abbotsbury would be to watch Violet die without even the palliative that expert nursing and medical advice could give her. In October a wooden bungalow was purchased on the outskirts of Yateley in Hampshire—thirty-five miles from London and within easy reach of Midhurst. Soon the sound of the surf booming on the Chesil Bank would be heard no more.

For my father it must have seemed like a willed descent into the catacombs. The Coastguard Station, when he had first found it, had been lit with 'the gleam that never was on land or sea'. The first two years he spent there had been among the happiest and most productive of his life. To his brother Richard they were 'halcyon days' filled with sunshine and laughter and the contentment which comes from hard and satisfying work. So many of father's cherished dreams seemed to have come true at last. He was married to a beautiful girl who loved him with an adoration beyond all computation; he had become an acknowledged master of his chosen métier and *Keats and Shakespeare*, *The Life of Jesus* and *The Adelphi* were the proof of it; the baby daughter he had always longed for was an ever-present and wholly enchanting reality; true friends were close at hand; he had a small boat and a seine net—once they had even scooped 'a miraculous draught of fishes', over a thousand mackerel in one scoop; there was the sea and the whole of the unspoilt Dorset countryside theirs for the taking. Small wonder that, in the years to come, as the shadows darkened around him, those brief Abbotsbury years seemed to glitter ever brighter in retrospect until they took their rightful place beside the golden months at the Villa Pauline in Bandol where he had first discovered true happiness with Katherine.

3 At the time of the move to Yateley I was two and a half years old, my sister three and a half. The bungalow was called South Acre and it was to be our home for the next two and a half years. No sooner were we installed than my father and his brother set about improving the garden. There was obviously plenty of scope for improvement since photographs show the house to have stood in an acre of rough pasture in which thistles and ragweed rose as high as the windowsills. Beyond, sloping gradually up to a blue line of distant woodland was an enormous cornfield. No doubt it was not as vast as I remember it, but when I first set eyes on it that field seemed to stretch to the world's end.

Shortly after our arrival at South Acre I expressed my disapproval of existence in general by becoming ill again. Once more the spectre of T.B. was conjured up and I believe I was packed off to the Midhurst sanatorium. I say 'I believe' because my mental censor has carefully erased all specific recollection of this period other than a recurrent nightmare which haunted me for years of being trapped and abandoned inside a white-barred cage from which there was no escape. I was also dimly conscious that it was my father who had put me in it.

By the spring of the following year I was back at Yateley and for this I had Dr James Young to thank. 'Jimmy' Young, in whose arms Katherine Mansfield had died at the Gurdjieff Institute in Fontainebleau, was an altogether remarkable man. I remember my father once saying of him that he was "too intelligent to be a doctor", by which he meant, I imagine, that Jimmy found it difficult to suffer fools gladly for any length of time. More than once he ruined excellent chances of making his fortune by blurting out the truth about his professional colleagues. By keeping his mind 'a thoroughfare for all thoughts and not a select party' he earned himself the enmity of the less gifted and a reputation for erratic brilliance as a diagnostician. But above all, Jimmy was a pragmatist. If it worked—no matter how unorthodox it was—he was for it. Again and again he broke all the rules in order to give a patient a reason for living. His favourite word was 'humbug', and his vocabulary of swearwords was so enormous and so varied that I once listened enthralled as he rounded on my raging stepmother and reeled off a string of scatological epithets that reduced even her to stunned silence. In facial appearance he bore a vague resemblance to the film actor Tyrone Power; dark hair slicked back, a rugged, walnut brown face, and humorous eyes. He drank like a fish. It is more than likely that I owe him my life.

It is from the time of my return to South Acre that the various tiny trickles of memory begin to unite into a coherent stream, though my mother still remains conspicuously absent from any of them. Jimmy had insisted that to keep me exiled in the sanatorium was virtually tantamount to a death sentence. 'All he needs is love,' he pronounced roundly. The trouble was there was not much of that invaluable commodity to spare around South Acre in 1929. My father was by now both physically and emotionally exhausted from the strain of nursing Violet, and Violet herself was three-quarters of the way along the road to her own Calvary. Nevertheless, fortunately for me, my father had sufficient faith in Jimmy's skill to entrust my well-being to him. And it worked. The white bars of the prison cage miraculously disappeared and I remember opening my eyes one day and gazing up into the blossom-laden branches of a tree in which a bird was singing. Higher still great silvery-white clouds were scudding like schooners across a sky of impossible blue. Warm sunshine tumbled down upon me through the dappling leaves. I turned my head and saw my sister peering in at me through the side of the wooden cot in which I was lying. She put her hand through the bars and touched my face. It was like waking up from a bad dream.

To look after the two of us my father had engaged a woman we came to know as 'Nanna'. If she had another name I have never discovered what it was. I remember her only as a grey-haired, kindly soul who wore a white bib apron. I suspect that she was not particularly efficient and I'm sure we made life as difficult for her as we possibly could. She used to concoct a mysterious linctus from brown sugar and onions and her hair-pins were always dropping out. One summer evening—it must have been in 1930—after Weg and I had been bathed and put to bed, we climbed out of our bedroom window and disported ourselves on the croquet lawn which had by now replaced the thistles and ragwort. Nanna soon spotted us and emerged in pursuit, billowing and clucking like a mother hen. For several minutes we dodged and scampered up and down, easily evading her attempts to recapture us, until suddenly I realized that she was weeping. I suppose it was the first time I had ever seen a grown-up in tears and the effect upon me was profoundly shocking. I ran to her and flung my arms round her and hugged her to me crying: 'You mustn't! You mustn't! Stop it, Nanna! Stop it!'

'Oh, you're wicked, wicked children,' she panted. 'If Sister's seen you, I'll be dismissed. Get along in with you before you catch your deaths.' And producing a large white handkerchief she trumpeted loudly into it and shooed us back indoors.

The 'Sister' she referred to was a certain Sister Verity who had been taken on ostensibly to nurse my mother. She stretches like a long black shadow across those days at Yateley. There was some sort of feud between her and Nanna which I never fully understood but I realized enough to know that for all her bumbling and complaining, Nanna was essentially kind-hearted and forgiving, whereas Sister Verity was a terror. Nanna was afraid of her and, looking back, I can see that there was something definitely 'kinky' about Sister Verity. I remember how, on the occasions when she bathed us, she contrived to pinch us, little sharp venomous nips with her fingernails, always in places where it would not show. She had completely black eyes so that it was impossible to tell where the pupils ended and the irises began and she used to turn these on us and give us a thin, thoughtful mouth-smile at the very moment she was about to stick her nails into us.

One day she produced a little whippy cane and swished it through the air till it sang like a mosquito. Then she smiled her thin, cold smile and came slowly towards me. I backed away from her until I was pressed up against the bedroom wall. 'Col's been a naughty boy,' she mused. 'We know what must be done with naughty boys, don't we?' and again the little cane whistled spitefully. I was too terrified to say a word. I knew I was going to be sick, and I knew that if I *was* sick she would have an excuse for whipping me. Fortunately at that moment we both heard my father's car drive up. I was so relieved I promptly wet myself.

How long Sister Verity's reign of terror lasted I have no idea. The strange thing is that neither Weg nor I ever complained to my father about her. Somehow she had succeeded in instilling into us both the conviction that we could never escape her. When Nanna discovered the existence of that cane she took it and hid it. I was petrified. At the age of four I recognized an authentic act of hubris when I saw one. Sister Verity was Fate and no one could escape that.

Ultimately she excelled herself and, I suspect, brought about her own dismissal. One night my sister and I were asleep, sharing a bed, when we were woken by the door squeaking open. We peered up over the bedclothes and, rigid with fright, saw an awful white shape which moaned and gibbered at us over the foot of the bed. With a shriek of terror we clutched at one another. A moment later the bedroom light clicked on and there was Sister Verity demanding coldly to know what all the fuss was about. When Nanna hurried in Sister told her that we had had a nightmare or something. Weg and I were not capable of giving any coherent account of our experience. But for once Nanna had the courage of her suspicions, and the next day she went and had a long talk to my father. What she told him must have convinced him because by lunch time Sister Verity had been sent packing. Unfortunately her memory remained.

4 NOW, as I look back, I can see quite clearly that a firm pattern had already become established for me. Life, I understood, was to be full of quite appalling experiences and there was absolutely nothing I could do to avoid them. I was out on my own. Things would happen to me and I would perhaps endure them, but I would never be able to believe in advance that I *would* endure them. Furthermore there was no court of appeal. True, there was my father, but already I had sensed in him that quality of remoteness, of withdrawing from me, that I could recognize even though I could not understand its cause. Having read his journal covering the last year of Violet's illness I realize that he really had reached the end of his emotional tether. The same phrases occur day after day like the dull tolling of a minute bell: "11.15. Violet sick. Cleaned up." "How *tired* I am of listening to that cough of Violet's!" "V. sick." "Her cough seems to vibrate on my spine." And with it the anguish and the guilt of knowing there was nothing he could do to prevent the inevitable outcome. His faith in a miracle had long since been leached away. "V. was looking exhausted when I went in; but glad to see me—a half an hour early. She said that when she felt bad before the aspirin 'death seemed so commonplace, like the door of a public lavatory. Everything was somehow blunted: there was nothing magnificent about death.' A little while after that I broke down, horribly . . ."

It was during this dark period that Max Plowman entered our lives. Curiously enough it seems that I was instrumental in bringing Max and my father together. The Plowmans' adored eleven year old son Timothy had died in 1928. Hearing that I too was seriously ill, Max felt drawn by a bond of sympathy towards my father. By then, understandably, my father was hypersensitive to any new human contact. Like a hurt animal he simply wanted "to crawl away and lick his own wounds in darkness." But Max had a genius for friendship and in the end the sheer sincerity of his sympathy carried the day.

Having won my father's confidence, he and his wife Dorothy set about lightening the Yateley burden. Almost their first act of generosity was to find a suitable replacement for Sister Verity. The girl they chose appeared to be ideal in every way—a simple, country lass, cheerful and spontaneous, who seemed to bring sunshine into a house of the dead. At once a new note can be detected in my father's journals and, looking back to those days he was later to write of May 1930:

"Such life as I had not heard for years came echoing every day from Violet's room. There was the same dull hammering of her cough upon my spine, but it was now only the undertone —forgotten in laughter. And Betty's life seemed to pour into Violet's veins. She worked the livelong day gaily; she never went out and never complained: she was happy. And she loved Violet with a careless, living love; whereas my love was the careful, anguished love that is death."

The irony is that if, during that same month, my father had been able to peep a few years into the future, Violet or no Violet, Betty would have left on the next train. Four months later, had she done so, he would have chased after her and brought her back.

As far as my sister and I were able to judge, things had definitely improved. Since our immediate standard of reference was Sister Verity this was understandable. Betty had a 'no nonsense' way about her which at least let you know where you stood. I learnt this very early in our acquaintance. Since I had now fully recovered my health, such attention as I had been able to claim by reason of my illness was diverted elsewhere. Once again I began to view Weg as the chief obstacle in my path towards my parents' affection. My methods of dealing with the problem were lacking in subtlety but not undramatic. One day I thumped her over the head with a croquet mallet. This certainly gained me some attention, but it hardly helped towards winning my father's love. On another occasion I bit her on the cheek. Betty, who happened to be on the scene, promptly caught hold of my arm and bit me too—hard. This awakened in me a healthy respect for Betty's methods. It also cured me, temporarily at least, of biting. It shames me to record that even after this assault it was Weg who stuck up for me. My father noted the event thus: "Today Col bit Weg on the face: a really horrid mark. Miss Cockbayne (Betty) said to Weg while she was still crying, 'Col isn't a little boy, he's a little beast.' Weg answered: 'He isn't a little beast, he's a little boy; and I love him.'"

It must have been at about this time that I discovered why my sister was so much nicer than I was. She had been Christened and I hadn't! I had no idea what it meant but it marked a frontier between us. Probably I saw in it an explanation of why my father preferred her to me. When I informed her of my discovery her brown eyes went very round as they always used to at my revelations. 'Oh, that's just sil-ly,' she said. 'You're only naugh-ty because you're a boy-ee.' This aspect of the situation had not occurred to me. It set me pondering on the essential differences between the sexes. Boys wore trousers and peed standing up and girls wore frocks and peed squatting down. Boys had their hair cut short and could throw stones straighter than girls. Girls liked picking flowers. But was there something else? There had been a quiet confidence about Weg's assertion that made me think there must be. Perhaps it was my gender which was always urging me on to experiment, to caper on the brink of disaster. At times it must have seemed to Weg that I had a positive death wish. One instance will suffice as illustration. My father owned a car. It was called a Trojan. It had solid tyres and was shaped rather like a boat. Violet had nicknamed it 'The Flying Bedstead', and when it broke down my father's method of dealing with it was to get out, walk twenty or thirty yards up the road away from it, pick up a stone and shy it at the intractable beast. He swore the method worked like a charm. Naturally Weg and I were forbidden to go near this monster. Perhaps my father feared it might get its own back on him by savaging us.

One day, prompted by God knows what wild Freudian urge to experiment, I crept up to 'The Flying Bedstead' and thrust a large carrot up its capacious exhaust pipe. Shortly afterwards my father summoned me to accompany him to the local golf course. His bag of clubs was heaved aboard and I after it. My father fiddled with the choke, adjusted the spark lever, then stooped over the bonnet and cranked the starting handle. Nothing happened. He muttered something and cranked again. Still nothing. He frowned, made a few further adjustments to the controls and tried for the third time. The engine coughed once and then, with a truly thunderous report, my carrot was expelled amid a cloud of blue smoke to crash up against the wooden door of the potting shed. My father's astonished face peered up over the bonnet—his glasses knocked awry—and he gazed around him in bewilderment. 'What the devil was that?' he demanded. I shook my head in a parody of wide-eyed innocence that could have deceived no one except him. Fortunately for me the car started at the very next go.

Those trips to the golf course were a regular feature of our lives at this time. My father used golf as a drug to stop him thinking about Violet. He had a natural aptitude for ball games which I was to inherit from him. He equipped Weg and myself with a cut-down club apiece and we accompanied him on his rounds. Occasionally Jimmy Young joined us and the hazards of the East Berkshire golf course called forth all the riches of his remarkable vocabulary. On one occasion when he had had half a dozen swipes at a deeply bunkered ball he summoned me to him and told me to hit the bloody thing for him. Only too happy to oblige I scrambled down into the bunker, swung my sawn-off niblick, eyed the ball and clipped it sweetly out to within a yard of the pin. Jimmy laughed so much he missed the putt.

Most of the land around Yateley has now been built over, but between the wars it was still proper country in which slow shire horses jingled musically as they dragged the ploughs, hares gambolled on the commons, and the woodland walks were secret and strangely still. There was even a white-aproned muffin man who used to stride past South Acre once a week carrying a wooden tray on his head and ringing a hand-bell. 'Moof-ins!' he called. 'Fresh moof-ins!' until his voice faded away in the distance and his bell mingled with the birdsong.

Not that it was always so tranquil. One day my father took us for a walk down the lane towards the two bridges which Weg and I had claimed for our own, our favourite pastime being to race sticks down the stream and see which one emerged first from under the arch. On our way home we heard a fearsome grinding and clattering, unlike any sound I had heard before. It seemed to be coming along the road behind us. I glanced back apprehensively and saw what I now realize was a convoy of whippet tanks from Aldershot clanking after us. 'It's quite all right,' my father assured us. 'They won't hurt us.'

I longed to believe him, but I recognized evil when I saw it. With a wail of terror I released my hand from his and fled. Nor did I stop running until I reached the sanctuary of South Acre where I rushed indoors and hid myself under the bed. When Weg appeared she said: 'Why did you run away? Dadda said they wouldn't hurt us and so they didn't.' I was not then familiar with the expression 'Perfect love casteth out fear' but I recognized a difference in kind between her faith and mine. 'I wanted to go on the lav,' I lied brazenly. 'I wasn't running away.' I don't think she believed me.

On another occasion my father took us up to London to visit a friend of his. The name meant nothing to me but the memory of that visit is still extraordinarily vivid. Weg and I were shown into a long white room and told to 'amuse' ourselves. We looked around us with some trepidation. The floor was covered with toys: wooden bricks, toy soldiers, model railways, all scattered in profusion. While we were gazing at them doubtfully, a door at the far end of the room opened quietly and a small, plump-faced man with the bluest eyes I had ever seen came in on his hands and knees. His head was just about on the same level as ours. 'Hello,' he said. 'So you've come to play with me, have you? That's fine, fine.'

In a twinkling he had us both organized. I was to be the commander of the Red army; Weg of the Blue; while he rushed round frantically winding up clockwork trains, constructing bridges and fortifications, firing pencils out of toy cannons. It was all highly hysterical—quite unlike any grown-up behaviour

I had ever known. And then, almost without our noticing it, he had slipped away.

Eventually my father appeared to collect us and take us home. The little plump man appeared once again and handed us each a book. Weg's was called *Floor Games*, mine *Little Wars*. Inside each he had written our names and underneath 'With love from H. G. Wells.' Throughout my childhood I used those books just as their author would have wished them to be used—as practical hand-books. I drew and scribbled all over them and it was years before I was able to link them and that magical afternoon with the author of what had by then become one of my favourite novels *The War of the Worlds*.

5

THROUGHOUT 1930 the Plowmans came to play an ever larger part in our lives. Max's wife, Dorothy, I remember as a nebulous, wispy figure who wore her hair bound round her head in a braid. Rather like a younger version of Nanna in some ways, she had a tendency to cluck and fuss over me that I found oddly disquieting. It occurs to me now that perhaps I was reacting to her desire to see me not as I truly was but as some sort of reincarnation of her own dead son. But she was kindness itself and I can recall no cross word she ever spoke to me. Why then, I wonder, is she not more distinct in my memory? She exists for me like a figure in an out-of-focus photograph. By concentrating hard I can make out the traces of a slightly worried frown and an impression of someone who always seemed to be trying to recall where she had mislaid something. No doubt I do her an injustice, for at this particular time she must have found herself in an extraordinarily difficult position.

What was happening was that Max had become convinced that it was within his power to restore Violet to health. He had the spiritual faith which can move mountains and such was the strength of his conviction that he was able to persuade my father to let him try. For my father it must have been like shrugging off a well-nigh intolerable burden, and he believed that, had he himself been able to muster up Max's sort of faith, then Violet might indeed have pulled round. As it was his experience with Katherine had engendered within him a sort of granite fatalism. Try as he would he *knew* in his heart of hearts that Violet would die and, what is worse, he believed that it was his stony conviction which was making her death inevitable. This, I think, was the only time in his life when he genuinely longed for death himself—as a release from a struggle which had lost all meaning for him.

At the end of December he went away with Jimmy Young for a few days' rest leaving Violet in the care of the Plowmans. He returned to find "a different woman". Max's faith had apparently worked the trick—or worked *a* trick. Violet's confidence in herself was completely restored, but at a price. The price was the transfer of her love from my father to Max. By responding to her—loving her—for the natural and completely spontaneous girl she was in a way in which my father was no longer capable of doing—if, indeed, he ever had been—Max had taken the burden upon himself. My father's journal entry for January 6th, 1931, describing this, ends with the words: "I feel very empty." The next day he recalls Katherine's state of mind in August–September 1922 and compares it ominously with Violet's. Belief in miracles was no longer within his power.

It is not surprising—though I think my father *was* surprised—that, with Violet's emotional hunger being fed by someone else, he himself no longer felt bound to her in the same way. In a series of long letters and conversations with Max he tried to come to terms with his own feelings towards Violet, and Max responded by trying to illuminate my father's marriage experiences from his own. Finally, after an even more tortuous piece of self-analysis than usual, my father quotes with wry relief and approval, a typical remark of Betty's: 'You people take life too seriously, too damn seriously.' Coming when it does that entry is not without significance.

The Plowmans had suggested that Violet should come up to London and live with them in their house in Hampstead Garden Suburb. They felt that it was only by having her under their roof that they could wrap her round with the cocoon of their own faith in her recovery. My father acquiesced gladly, though his conviction, which he kept for his journal, was that what Max was doing was hastening Violet's end. "Of this I am certain," he wrote, "he is hurrying V. to physical death—to spiritual beatitude and physical death. I accept it, I am even glad of it, because I know there is nothing better to be done, nothing as good. But is he conscious of what he is doing? Or does he simply regard the body as of no account—death as a mere semblance? I remember his words: 'If I did not believe that Violet was going to get well, I should become untied'. I took him to mean, and he knew I took him to mean, 'well in body'. Will he say, when the inevitable end has come, he meant 'well in spirit'? Or will her death come as a crash to him?

"We are moving, being moved, irresistibly now to a consummation. Is Max putting a beautiful but illusory belief to the supreme test; or is he a wise, brave man making a dying girl happy? If the latter I admire and love him; if the former I simply love him. The beautiful but illusory belief is that Love has power to work miracles in the world of existence. And he pours forth love on Violet: real love, true love, of the individual Violet. And that is what she needs. That will carry her to the point at which death will be meaningless to her. Or, again, is he bearing my burden—loving Violet for me? One day I shall know. But now the love he gives V., Dorothy feels instinctively is being taken from her. Therefore, she feels, I must now turn to her. Max loves Violet: I must love her. That's very just and right; but I don't particularly feel the impulse. I suppose, if I were Max, I should. But being J.M.M. I don't . . ."

Alas, poor Dorothy. How could she realize that the kind of love—spiritual love—which she offered to my father was the very thing best suited to make him cringe away. He had had altogether too much of it and it sickened his soul. Understandably, he saw in such love only the seeds of death. He hungered for something which was not 'sicklied o'er with the pale cast of thought'; a relationship with a woman which offered warmth and comfort first and ecstasy maybe.

On February 18th Betty and he drove Violet up to Max's house, saw her safely installed, and returned to Yateley. Three days later there was an urgent phone call. My father drove back up to London, spent the next two nights with the Plowmans and realized finally that he had "no place with V. any more. They are doing everything; all her vital relation is with them: and I'm a fish miserably out of water."

The days dragged by. March came bringing bitterly cold east winds and faded blue skies. My father travelled regularly up to London and found Violet "radiantly happy" but it was a radiance he recognized only too well from that last disastrous visit to Fontainebleau eight years before—the brilliant flaring up of the doomed spirit just before the end. Well might Violet say that she felt "the disease didn't belong to her". In the truest sense it didn't; but it was proving just as lethal as if it did.

It is at this point that Weg and I were taken up to see Violet. I remember standing at the foot of the bed and gazing at her. I am not even sure that I knew who she was. Pale spring sunshine was slanting in through the window. Outside a branch with green and silvery leaves fluttered and swayed up and down. A plate of dark blue grapes was standing on the table beside the bed. I looked from the grapes to the woman lying propped against the white pillows and her eyes seemed to me as dark as the grapes. She reached out, broke off a little bunch of the fruit and handed it to me. In the sunbeams her thin fingers appeared almost translucent. As I took the grapes from her she began to cough—a sort of dry, hiccupping cough—and I was propelled gently out of the room. If she spoke to me I have forgotten it.

I have often wondered what her feelings were towards me. The journal she kept has long since vanished and there is no reference to me in the extracts my father quotes from it. She had given me life and had nothing left to spare for me. That was no fault of hers. Those who knew her all speak of her joyous spontaneity, her ability to respond totally to experience and to identify with whoever she was with. How cheated she must have felt, knowing how much she had within her to give and that there were no means left to her by which to give it. I could never manage to come to terms with her at all. As a boy the only photograph of her I possessed was of a brown-eyed little girl peeping out from behind a tree. 'That's your mother,' they said. I peered at it in disbelief and felt the world lurch around me. 'When she was your age,' they added. But the damage was already done. Now I am twice as old as she was when she gave birth to me and the illusion still persists. I have *always* felt myself to be older than she was.

6

VIOLET died at 3.40 a.m. on Sunday March 29th, 1931, but for my father it could only have marked the end of her posthumous existence. Six weeks previously he and Betty had become lovers. Weg had apparently drawn my attention to a change in their relationship when, peering out through the bedroom window into the rose garden at Yateley, she had glimpsed something which must have made her eyes pop. 'Col!' she cried, 'Dadda is cuddling Miss Cockbayne!'

I am sure my immediate reaction must have been ribald laughter. Underneath I would have felt it was a very good thing. I was all for kissing and cuddling. The only trouble was there was never enough of it. Weg, I imagine, was less sanguine. Did she suspect, even then, that Betty would brook no rivals for my father's affection? Or was she simply acknowledging that his love for her could never be quite the same? Either way she was going to be the loser. Me? What had I to lose?

My father was quite sure he had done the right thing. In his journal entry for March 8th he observes: "Difficulties there will be; but that can't be helped. Right down in my soul I know that this is a good thing that has happened to me: to be loved by a warm, generous, natural, healthy woman." I very much doubt whether he had fully considered all the possible connotations of the word 'natural' when he penned that sentence. In fact I'm quite certain that he had no idea what a genuinely 'natural' woman might amount to. He was soon to find out.

Two days later he told Max what had happened. Max took the news with commendable phlegm. 'That's a surprise,' he said. 'Since when, John?' After my father had told him he considered for a while then said: 'No, I'm not really surprised.'

The truth is that Max was more than surprised; he was profoundly shaken. All along he had, as he explained in a letter to my father, been hoping "that I could sustain her (Violet) and gradually release her imagination so that she would be able to pick up her life again and draw together the broken threads on the imaginative plane that were so pitifully snapped on the instinctive. All the weeks she was with us I lived with the idea of restoring her health of mind, which was synonymous to me with restoring her to you. But what I discovered with a shock after she had died, was that she had, for you, died in life, and that while she lived you had really given her up in your affectional life . . ." The note of hurt in that letter of Max's is certainly understandable, nevertheless I think it betrays a failure to come to imaginative grips with what my father had had to endure up to the point when he surrendered Violet. Ever since he had brought her back from Midhurst to Abbotsbury he had devoted his life to nursing her to the exclusion of his work and his children. In failing to appreciate my father's true state—"The primitive physical vitality from which our power to love is nourished was failing within me"—Max shows, I believe, that my father's assessment of his motives was essentially correct: he was indeed trying to sustain the 'beautiful illusion' that 'Love has power to work miracles in the world of existence'.

It says everything for Max that his abiding affection for my father was able to survive even this earthquake. He 'loved the man', and until Max's own death some ten years later my father's response was to love him back with the kind of love which 'looks on tempests and is never shaken'. "Of all the men I have ever known," he was to write on the day after Max's death in 1941, "Max was the most warm-hearted, the most understanding, the most loving . . . When all the world was reeling about me, when all the things and all the people I had believed in fell away and I had to perform acts which I knew to be absolutely mad in the eyes of the world—Max stayed still, and accepted, and understood . . ."

The feeling behind those words rings absolutely true but, even so, there was certainly one occasion when Max, though he 'stayed still' and 'accepted' can hardly be claimed to have 'understood'. This was when, some three weeks after Violet's funeral, my father informed him that he intended to marry Betty. Such an act was, in Max's view, bordering upon lunacy, and something in the almost universal hostility the proposal aroused among his friends must have penetrated my father. It did not, alas, deter him, but it gave him a few moments' uneasiness nonetheless; for Betty had already begun to show signs of a temperament which, like her unashamed sensuality, was something quite new in his experience. On the very day before he told Max of his intention, he is confiding to his journal that "I felt very dubious on Wednesday night. Perhaps it was all stupid and mistaken; perhaps I had better go away and live with the children alone, and put up with the horror of 'well-meaning', scheming, sympathetic females. . . ."

Some part of that 'dubiousness' may well have sprung from a strange interview with Betty's father—a farmer at Stoneleigh, near Banbury. At their first meeting he had found occasion to draw my father aside and ask him quietly if he knew what he was doing. It was a shrewd question and not one which my father found possible to answer other than with: 'Yes, I think so. Why?'

'You know she's got the devil of a temper on her?'

My father, I suspect, must have responded to this with one of his notoriously enigmatic smiles.

Mr Cockbayne sighed. 'Well, I wouldn't like any man to think I hadn't given him fair warning of what he was letting himself in for.'

By those words he seemed to lift the whole enterprise on to an almost Lawrentian plane. It was as if the symbolic 'man/woman relationship' which was to preoccupy my father off and on until his death had shown itself to him outside his printed page for the first time. Violet and Katherine he had always thought of first and foremost as 'Violet' and 'Katherine'—as feminine, certainly, but above all as rational, human individuals. Betty was beginning to look as if she might prove to be something different in kind rather than in degree. I've occasionally wondered whether this did not contribute a major portion of her original attraction for him.

The one thing which Betty was not interested in at any price was 'spiritual love'. This made excellent sense to my father who had always been "travailed by a longing for physical love". All his life he had hoped it would be possible to form a love relationship with a woman who could share both his "thought adventures" and his bed with equal (and mutual) satisfaction. Experience had taught him otherwise. Very well then, from now on he would voyage through his strange seas of thought alone. His third marriage was to be "a simpler kind of love", supremely natural and full of warmth and tenderness. Perhaps he took Betty into his confidence about this dream but somehow I'm inclined to doubt it. In its own way it was just as much a "thought adventure" as all the others.

In the period immediately following our mother's funeral my sister and I seem to have led a somewhat nomadic existence. We spent some weeks with the Plowmans at a cottage on the Isle of Wight during which Dorothy introduced us to the nonsense verses of Edward Lear and we both took strong exception to the 'bossiness' of Max's eleven year old son, Piers. He ordered us about as though we were his vassals. On one occasion when we were all picking mushrooms on St Boniface Down above Ventnor he earned Weg's censure by rejecting all the ones I picked as being hopelessly inferior. She promptly attacked him with her wooden spade. He was too astonished to retaliate, though I'm sure he must have levelled the scores later.

Another temporary resting place was with the Cockbaynes at Stoneleigh. This was altogether more to our taste because there we were allowed to play with water and mud to our hearts' content. One day Betty's father went off to Banbury and told his dog to be sure and keep an eye on us while he was away. His return was delayed till well on into the afternoon, but such was the dog's loyalty that he would allow no one to approach us. Molly, Betty's sister whom we both adored, brought our lunch out into the yard and called out to us that we'd have to fetch it ourselves because 'that Jess won't let me near you till Dad gets back'.

It was during that stay that I had an unnerving experience. One of the men at the farm took me off with him into the fields while he chopped thistles. For this job he used a special sort of heavy mattock with a razor-sharp edge. His method was to plant a foot on either side of the thistle and chop down, severing the root a couple of inches below the soil. Either he got careless or the blade struck some invisible obstruction underground and was diverted sideways for the next thing I knew was that he was sitting on the ground gripping his leather-gaitered calf in both hands while the bright red blood came welling up in spurts between his fingers. 'Run on back home, boy,' he panted. 'Tell 'em what's happened. I dursent let go. Quick now! Run like the wind!'

I took one last glance at his pale, drawn face and fled. I suppose I must have succeeded in finding someone because my memory of the incident ends there, as does any further recollection of my stay at Stoneleigh.

What with one thing and another I seem to have become

something of a handful at this period in my life. On my return to Yateley I reverted to being Weg's 'naught-ee boy-ee'. One entry in my father's journal for June 6th, 1931 reads: "I hear that Col behaved like a scamp while I was away, throwing stones at Weg, and at 'The Flying Bedstead', and biting Pottinger. He really is becoming rather a problem: for which the responsibility on me is heavy." Perhaps fortunately for me I was one of the responsibilities he felt only spasmodically.

For some time past my father's thoughts had been revolving round quitting Yateley. He had, as he put it—"more or less decided to buy a largish house and settle myself—a house where the children, and others to come, may run wild and be full of memories . . ." It was while Weg and I were at Stoneleigh that he and Betty had set out on a journey of exploration which was to take them for 1300 miles backwards and forwards through Norfolk and Suffolk. The house they eventually found seemed ideal in every respect. Certainly it was destined to leave us with many memories.

7

MY father bought the Old Rectory, Larling, for £1,000. It was almost exactly one hundred years old, late Georgian in style, and wholly beautiful. It lay on the western edge of the Norfolk brecklands—that mysterious expanse of sandy, brackeny heath, dotted with pine trees whose trunks glow like rosy fingers in the setting sun. Eastwards stretched the heavy, sun-drowsed, Norfolk farmland through which wound the slow, reedy, river Thret. The house itself was completely surrounded by trees—huge, towering, beeches, elms and horse chestnuts—among whose leafy tops the wood-pigeons burbled all the summer long. Its grounds comprised vast shrubberies, a capacious meadow and a substantial walled garden. In all the property extended over some nine acres and, in its own way, was almost as isolated as the Old Coastguard

Station. In summer the house was totally invisible from the road and even in winter it could only be guessed at by glimpsing the sunlight winking from an upstairs window between the branches of the threadbare trees. To reach it you drove or trudged up a long, flint-paved driveway between thorns and holly hedges and, such was the strategic placing of the dense shrubberies, that the house remained concealed till the last possible moment. Then suddenly you were on a broad gravelled drive circling a lawn and the sun-faded, yellow-grey, brick house with its white door, white framed windows and dark, purply-blue, slated roof was there before you.

Weg and I were brought down to Larling by our Uncle Richard, having been parked with my father's parents in Brighton while the move from Yateley was being organized. We arrived in the afternoon. No sooner had I set eyes on the place than I knew I had seen it before. How or when I did not know, but I *knew*. For the next hour or so I simply surrendered myself to an assault of sensual impressions.

The house seemed enormous—compared to South Acre it *was* enormous—but what made the most profound impact upon me was the immense range of unfamiliar smells. They broke over me like so many waves. Fresh distemper and moist, scrubbed bricks in echoing sculleries and dairies; the intoxicating perfume of clove carnations in the walled garden; fizzing acid in the glass accumulator cells in the battery house; last year's rotting conker leaves drifted in the shrubberies; musty, sparrow-riddled reed thatch on the ancient summer-house; piles of spiralled pinewood shavings where the carpenter had been constructing dozens of new bookshelves. And everywhere, pervading every corner of the house, the delicious fragrance of freshly applied linseed-oil paint. So firmly did these scents imprint themselves upon my five year old memory that I have only to catch a whiff of one of them today and I am at once transported back in time to that first dreamlike encounter. It was as if the house and the garden were opening invisible arms and enfolding me. For the first time in my life I felt instinctively that I had come home.

But that first night, lying alone in a strange bed upstairs in the nursery, I heard the breeze snuffling among the leafy branches outside the open window; I saw the curtains tremble as though they were alive; and I called out in alarm. There was a patter of naked feet on the linoleum; the door handle rattled, clicked, and the door to the adjoining room opened. A stout indomitable little figure in button-up pyjamas marched in and asked me what was the matter.

I pointed timorously to the quivering curtains. 'There's something going to pounce on me.'

'I'll get it,' said my sister. 'Don't you worry.'

Boldly she picked up a pair of iron fire tongs as long as herself; fearlessly she attacked the curtains. 'There,' she panted, 'that's done for it. Now go to sleep like a brave little man.' She replaced the tongs, tucked me in firmly and kissed me. She was then all of six years old.

To teach the two of us my father had engaged as governess Emily Tomlinson, the sister of the author H. M. Tomlinson, our neighbour at the Coastguard Station. She was the first of a series of such ladies, none of whom stayed the course very long. In retrospect they have all merged into one—a sort of kindly, bewildered, grey-haired, composite soul who taught us how to tell the time by means of clock faces which we constructed under her guidance out of yellow Gold Flake cigarette boxes. There were always plenty of these available because my father smoked like a prairie fire. The only other lesson I recall was the assembling of an elaborate frieze on the theme of Ancient Egypt. Weg and I laboriously traced and scissored out silhouettes of *fellahin* from brown paper and pasted them on with Gloy. I thus discovered that the Ancient Egyptians manufactured their bricks out of mud and straw. I am still awaiting an opportunity to make use of this information.

The reason our governesses did not last long was that Betty invariably took against them, and once Betty took against anyone their fate was sealed. It became a simple question of how long they could hold out. Whether her rancour stemmed from jealousy of their intellectual pretensions I do not know, but I suspect it was chiefly because they were women. Whatever the reason, these unfortunate creatures inadvertently introduced a new and significant word into our vocabulary. The word was 'row' and it rhymed with 'pow!' Rows soon became the most dreaded events in our lives. There was something almost supernatural about them. They could appear like a cloud out of a completely blue sky. One minute nothing: the next, Jove's thunderbolts were crashing about your ears. When she was in full spate Betty was awe-inspiring—a truly elemental fury. To attempt to reason with her was impossible. She despised reason. To try to follow her line of thought when she was working herself up into a rage was to risk permanent dislocation of the intellect. Not only that, at such times she exuded a sort of black, demonic force of pure annihilation like a psychic miasma. Confronted with it the strongest men became mere straws. I recall once seeing a neighbour of ours who stood six foot two and had won the M.C. on the Somme emerging grey-faced and trembling from a brief encounter with her. 'Jesus Christ!' he muttered as he caught sight of me peeping apprehensively at him from the shelter of the stairwell. 'Your poor bloody father!'

During our first months at Larling the rows were relatively mild. They did not seem so at the time of course, but compared with what was to come they were as a gentle zephyr beside a hurricane. Their effect upon me was to sharpen immeasurably my sense of apprehension. Early in life I learnt the truth of Doctor Johnson's observation that: 'When a man knows he is to be hanged in a fortnight it concentrates his mind wonderfully.' I became both a highly skilled liar and an adept at merging myself into the landscape whenever trouble threatened. Furthermore I discovered in myself a talent for wild clowning, an innate ability to make grown-up people laugh. Not only 'people'—I could even make Betty laugh! And, providing I could catch it in time, I could sometimes even manage to defuse a row before it exploded. It did not always work but it worked often enough to make the effort worth while. I cultivated my gift for mimicry and made a speciality of taking-off whoever she was gunning for at that moment. More than once, ascending ever higher by great upward leaps of inspired fantasy like some intoxicated chamois, I disappeared into the clouds from which I promptly tumbled in tears of nervous hysteria. Betty's phrase for these performances of mine was 'acting the giddy goat'. It wasn't such a bad description either.

It would be wholly unfair to Betty to give the impression that she was never anything but a virago. From those early years at Larling I can recall plenty of times of true gaiety and happiness. Admittedly they were to become ever rarer oases in the desert but one remembered them and never quite gave up hope. Furthermore it soon became apparent to me that Betty didn't 'have it in' for me in quite the same way as she did for my sister. At first I accepted this as just another piece of inexplicable good fortune, but then it dawned on me that it was somehow related to the fact that my father liked Weg more than he liked me. Since I already knew this to be an edict of life, the discovery did not particularly disturb me. In a detached sort of way I was even able to feel sorry for Weg. But in a world where it was every creature for himself and the devil take the hindermost, such consolation as I was able to offer her was inevitably tempered with self-interest.

Our household at this time consisted of ourselves; a young maid called Myrtle who was permanently homesick and spent much of her time weeping quietly up in her bedroom; our governess; and 'Bodge' the gardener. Strictly speaking Bodge was not a member of the household since he lived three miles away in the village of Shropham and rode over every day on his bicycle, but to all intents and purposes he belonged to us. His proper name was Cyril Hewitt and he was one of that fortunate breed of men whose destiny it is to be loved. A truly gentle man, he adored children and really understood them, which is perhaps but to say that he never talked down to us and seemed able to identify with us quite effortlessly.

I imagine that he must have been in his early thirties when he first came to work for us. Certainly he had been in the war because he sometimes told us funny stories of his adventures in the horse-drawn artillery. I once asked him if he had seen anyone killed. He just smiled and said: 'Ah, that I have, but it don't do any good to think about it,' and adroitly changed the subject.

When our cat Spider broke her leg in a trap and my father said sombrely that she might have to be 'put down' we ran to Bodge for succour. 'Ah, she'll mend all right, m'old dear,' he said. 'I'll fix her up.' He did too. He slit a four inch length of garden hosepipe down one side, put the broken limb inside it and bound it round with tarred string. Spider limped around for three weeks and then Bodge took the splint off. To our delight she was completely healed.

Over the years he had to repeat the treatment several times. Spider grew to look increasingly battered but it did not seem to diminish either her agility or her attractions for the local toms. She produced litter after litter of kittens and these too Bodge was called upon to deal with. Finally in desperation, Spider took her pregnant self off to the woods and succeeded in raising a family undetected. We discovered them eventually in a lair half way up inside a hollow tree. Spider looked at us as much as to say: 'If you *dare* . . .' But Bodge already knew all about them. 'I reckon she's earned herself this lot,' he said. 'They'll keep the rats down in Lumley's barn.'

In the afternoons he worked with my father in the garden and very soon there had sprung up between them a bond of genuine friendship based firmly upon mutual respect. Unlike Betty, my father was constitutionally incapable of treating an employee as anything but a human being with the same inalienable right "to be" as he claimed for himself. As Bodge himself once put it to me: 'Mr Murry never comes "the Master".' Probably too he was drawn to my father by natural male sympathy, for Bodge, no more than anyone else who was around, could escape being drawn into the maelstrom and he sometimes found himself right in the eye of it. Betty was frequently threatening to give him the sack but, fortunately for us all, he owed his allegiance to my father, and when Betty raged he contrived to keep out of her way till the storm had blown over. Quite soon it became impossible for us to imagine Larling without him.

In the autumn of our first year at the Old Rectory, it became obvious to me that Betty was pregnant. She had been talking about it for some time but it hadn't really sunk in. I knew women 'had' babies just as I knew that people 'had' the measles, but the actual process didn't interest me very much. Then one afternoon I happened to go into the bathroom when Betty was just getting out of the bath—no one ever locked our bathroom door unless we happened to have visitors staying—and I caught a full profile. 'Gosh!' I exclaimed. 'Is that it?'

Betty grinned amicably and agreed that it was.

'Well, how will it get out?' I demanded curiously.

'The same way as Dadda put it in. Through here.' She lifted one foot on to the rim of the bath and pointed between her legs.

I laughed. I was quite certain she was having me on.

'Don't you believe me?' she chuckled, towelling herself vigorously.

'Of course, I don't.'

'Why not?'

'Well, there isn't room.'

'Not now there isn't, but there will be. I'll stretch.'

'Really?'

She nodded. 'Yes. Really.'

And I believed her.

As a piece of practical Nature Study that lesson made a far more profound impression on me than any of those our hard-pressed governesses dished out. Try as I might I found the greatest difficulty in coping with anything the least bit abstract. Even when I was tracing letters in a Crown copy-book I found they had a distressing habit of wandering off on trails of their own devising. It was like the game of 'Whispers'—what went in at one end bore very little relation to what came out at the other. When one of our teachers regaled us with inspiring stories of a previous charge of hers who could read the newspaper at the age of three I felt instinctively that he was destined for a bad end. Besides, what need was there for me to learn to read when Weg was only too happy to read to me? In this as in all other intellectual accomplishments she was so immeasurably my superior that I simply opted out of the race. Why she could even do take-away sums in double figures; whereas I found the greatest difficulty in distinguishing between 5's and 8's and my rows of 9's had an infuriating way of leaning over further and further backwards like guardsmen overcome with heatstroke.

Once a month our lesson books were 'looked-over' by my father. I always found it a rather painful process. He turned the pages of mine glumly, no doubt recalling that when he was my age he had been construing Virgil or something equally fabulous, and then he sighed faintly. 'It's coming along nicely, old boy,' he said. 'Coming along very nicely.' I didn't believe him and I daresay he knew I didn't. I longed to win his approval but we both understood that it was never going to be in this way.

What I did have was an extremely retentive audial memory. I didn't realize I had and neither, it seems, did anyone else, but in no time at all I had most of our Beatrix Potter books off by heart and if Weg made a slip I was quick to correct her. Thus it came about that in the end I taught myself to read. For some reason which I have forgotten, Weg went away for a few days and I was left on my own. Unable to persuade anyone else to perform the chore of reading aloud to me I finally retired to the nursery with *The Tale of Mr. Jeremy Fisher* and 'read it' aloud to myself—'Once upon a time there was a frog called Mr. Jeremy Fisher; he lived in a little damp house amongst the buttercups at the edge of a pond. . . .' There was nothing to it! I even managed the word 'Ptolemy' and the bits in italics. I can still recall the sense of shivery excitement I felt when I was suddenly able to relate the shapes of the words on the page to the sounds they represented. I had made the connection and I had made it for myself.

I wonder what would have happened if I had run downstairs, dashed into my father's study and announced that I had taught myself to read. I am sure now that he would have been both astonished and delighted. Nevertheless I didn't do it. The reason, I am convinced, is that I couldn't bear the thought of his *not* being impressed. So in the end I told no one and it was not until Weg returned that the secret crept out. By then I was no longer excited by it.

My doubts as to my father's reaction to my achievement were founded on an incident which had occurred about a month previously. That morning I had been allowed to handle pen and ink for the first time. My pen had a shiny red handle and a silvery nib with the letters ACE MED stamped on it. I was told that MED stood for MEDIUM. The ink was Swan blue-black. I had made several interesting blots before I realized that it was not necessary to dip the pen right down into the bottom of the bottle each time. Gradually I mastered the technique though there was no noticeable improvement in the quality of my letters. Lessons over, the pen and ink were put away in the cupboard.

After lunch I was left to my own devices. I wandered up to the nursery, retrieved the pen and ink and set them out on the table. Then I took a sheet of clean white paper and sat down in front of it. At that point I noticed a half-open box of matches on the mantelpiece so I got up from my chair, brought the box over to the table, set it down and started to draw it.

My usual method of drawing was to rush in with all guns blazing but this time, conscious of the tricky new medium, I worked with extreme care and, as I proceeded, I realized I had made a momentous discovery. By drawing the box in a diamond shape rather than a rectangle I had been able to reproduce the illusion of 3-dimensions! I looked at my picture rather as the Virgin Mary might have regarded the infant Jesus. It was undoubtedly a masterpiece, but was I responsible for it? With a pounding heart I carefully limned in the row of exposed matches and gave each one a neatly rounded head in

Swan blue-black. Then I delicately shaded in the striking surface. With each stroke I sensed perfection blossoming beneath my ACE MED nib. The three-masted schooner on the outside of the box proved somewhat beyond me but it was easily identifiable from the words 'Ship Matches'. Finally, reluctantly, I laid down my pen and sucked the ink from my fingers. I recognized genuine inspiration when I was confronted with it. There was only one word to describe what I had produced: it was sublime.

I contemplated my picture from all angles and I couldn't find a flaw anywhere. Very well then, now it should compete for the supreme accolade—the veritable *prix d'or.* Holding the paper lightly but firmly by one corner I skipped downstairs and ran down the back yard to the granary workshop where I knew my father and my uncle were at work constructing bee-hives. As I mounted the steps I took another glance at my masterwork and was wholly reassured.

My father was fastening wooden sections together, brushing on the hot glue then tapping the joints together and pinning them into place. I waited till he had handed his completed section to my uncle then I strolled forward and casually—oh, so casually!—laid my paper on the bench before him and stepped back. He glanced round and gave me a faintly preoccupied smile. 'Hello, old boy. Come to help?'

I gave a shy sort of point towards my paper. 'Look,' I said.

Still with that same vague smile playing round his lips he glanced down and nodded. Then he picked up a piece of wood from the stack beside him and reached out for his glue brush.

I was simply stunned. Could he have *missed* it? 'I drew it,' I muttered. 'For you.' And even as I said the words I was assailed by an appalling doubt. I snatched up the paper and peered at it. 'Don't you see?' I cried. 'It's *open*!'

He smiled and nodded. 'Why so it is,' he said. 'Pass me that mallet, old boy.'

I handed him the mallet then turned and walked out. Before I'd reached the bottom of the granary steps I was crying so hard it's a wonder I didn't fall and break my neck. I almost wished I had.

8 AT about the time when I taught myself to read I became conscious that I possessed at least one very odd talent. Curiously enough it did not then strike me as being peculiar because I knew all about it—in fact, as far as I knew, I'd had it for at least as long as I could remember anything at all. This was the knack, or gift, of *déjà vu*—the sense of having already been in places or having heard things before. It was such a regular occurrence that, quite literally, I thought nothing of it. It took two special forms. The first, and the more common, was of simply recognizing a particular scene. Sometimes there were people present but most often it was just a fragment of landscape. It was this I had experienced most strongly when I had first set eyes on the Old Rectory and which had given me the overwhelming sensation of returning home. The second was rather more spectacular and was somehow connected with the surge of nervous exhilaration I experienced whenever I was 'acting the giddy goat'. It was as though I were riding a sort of invisible surf board and keeping just ahead of the crest of the breaking wave. I was aware of what people were going to say a moment before they said it. This allowed me a precious fraction of time in which to improvise smart answers, though really the whole process was purely instinctive, like making a perfect half-volley in tennis. It frequently got me into trouble for being cheeky.

A curious feature of the phenomenon was that I seemed to have no control over it whatsoever. Once I was fairly launched it was a question of 'I fell to earth, I knew not where'. On such occasions I said whatever came into my head and never bothered to ask myself how it had got there. I am now inclined to believe that what I was experiencing was some form of extra-sensory contact with those around me. Just *what* form I'm by no means sure, though certainly on one occasion I appear to have picked up like a wireless receiver an already conceived but unuttered thought.

The incident took place in the drawing room where my father was talking to an American guest. They were seated in armchairs on either side of the fireplace and I was sitting curled up on the sofa at the far end of the room. As far as I know I wasn't even listening to their conversation. Suddenly I piped up: 'You're going to say . . .' and delivered myself of some polysyllabic utterance which might as well have been in Hindustani for all I understood of it. The American turned to me with a look of such absolute astonishment on his face that I was appalled. Rather than suffer the inevitable consequences of being cheeky I bolted out through the french window and hid myself behind the summer house.

My odd faculty—if that is the right word for it—remained with me more or less undiminished till well on into adolescence, and I have often wondered whether it was not connected in some way with my lack of any true sense of identity. Nothing was easier for me than to slip outside myself and become wholly involved with whatever caught my attention. Sometimes the sensation was almost physical as when, lying on my back in the long grass and staring up at the clouds drifting overhead, I felt as though they were drawing me after them and that I could look down on myself from far above. At such times the tether that held me to my six year old self was tenuous indeed. I discovered, moreover, that I could establish what I can only describe as a willed 'connection' between myself and things outside myself. Being an eminently practical child I used this faculty to ensure that I hit things I aimed at when I flung stones. My powers in this capacity became almost legendary among my coevals at the village school. I could not explain *how* I did it but I called it 'feeling the line', by which I meant sensing the vital trajectory between my hand and the target. This ability too gradually diminished as I left my childhood behind me and by the time I had eventually become a member of the First XI of my final school, I had lost the magic and was just another good thrower.

My sister and I had entered the village school in October 1932. This was a direct result of my father's recent conversion to Socialism and, some would doubtless aver, the sole beneficial result. Naturally I was not aware of this at the time, though I gathered that Betty strongly disapproved of socialists as a species. She let it be known, *ad nauseam*, that though my father was free to do what he liked with his own two brats she wasn't going to have her child (i.e. my six months old step-sister Mary) 'turned into a bloody little bolshie'. Useless for my father to point out that Mary was just as much his child as hers. Betty's retort was invariable: 'She's mine! She came out of me and she's part of me!' Thus young Mary's destiny was sealed. She was to be both weapon and battlefield in a war of attrition that was to last, with only brief periods of truce, for the next ten years.

The village school at Larling consisted of two lofty rooms known, reasonably enough, as Big Room and Little Room. They were both painted institutional brown. There was also a cloakroom and that too was brown. The lavatories were out in the playground. The Little Room, in which I found myself, was the domain of a Miss Parrot. She was a large woman with a pillow bosom, hennaed hair and gold-rimmed glasses. Behind her back she was known to us all as 'Polly'.

I was by no means the youngest pupil in her class but I was certainly one of the smallest. I was placed in a double desk in the front row beside a boy in a grey, knitted jumper who whispered to me that his name was Gordon. 'Mine's Col,' I whispered back and promptly earned myself a rap on the head from Miss Parrot's long ruler. She then commanded us to be silent for prayers. I stole a peep behind me. The other children had all closed their eyes and clasped their hands under their noses so I did the same. 'Our Father,' said Miss Parrot briskly.

Like sprinters at the sound of the gun the class was off. 'Ar-Farth-wi-chartin-Evven-allo-be-Thy-Name-Thy-

Kingdumcum-Thywillbedone-on-earthasitisinEvven. . . .' I opened and closed my lips but I didn't deceive Miss Parrot even though I bawled 'Amen' as lustily as anyone. She frowned and leant down towards me. 'Don't you *know* The Lord's Prayer?' she asked in a shocked voice.

I shook my head and flushed pink to the tips of my ears. There was a sound of sipped breath from the expectant class behind me. What was going to happen? Perhaps the floor would open and the devil would swallow me up.

'Then you must learn it—*at once*!' said Miss Parrot, opening her eyes so wide that a rim of white appeared all around each iris.

The class breathed again. I nodded dumbly.

'Say "Yes, Miss,"' said Miss Parrot.

'Yes, Miss,' I murmured.

I was presented with a slate and a slate pencil and was moved to protest that at home I was used to pen and ink. I was made to understand that ink was a Big Room privilege. In the Little Room it was slates. I quickly mastered the new medium and under Gordon's expert tuition learnt how to produce an excruciating squeak by first rubbing the point of my slate pencil across my scalp and then applying it to my slate. My formal education had begun.

In the next few months I learnt how to make mats and napkin rings out of raffia; a poem about 'The friendly cow all red and white'; my seven times table; that 'i' goes before 'e' except after 'c'; that Britons never never never shall be slaves; and some interesting new facts about little girls. I also made numerous friends. Foremost among them was Gordon. He was the youngest member of the Batley family who lived in School Cottage. There were over a dozen Batley children. Mr Batley was a minute, taciturn little man who smoked a short clay pipe and did odd jobs including sweeping chimneys. All his children were terrified of him and referred to him as 'The Little Old Man'. His wife, Gordon's mother, was a sweet-tempered, grey-haired lady who, worn out with constant childbearing, now had something wrong with her legs and shuffled around the house with the aid of a stick. She wore extraordinary felt slippers which looked like tartan boats. She was known as 'our Mum'. None of her enormous brood of children, several of whom were already grown up and earning their own living, was taller than five foot two.

Gordon had an irrepressibly cheerful disposition and a severe cast in one golden-brown eye. Together we whipped wooden tops in the dusty road outside the Batleys' cottage; fired two-penny cap pistols; and constructed catapults. He also had a healthy disrespect for school and, during the season, would frequently absent himself and go off to earn pocket money by potato picking for the local farmers. He was saving up to buy himself an air-gun. We spent happy hours poring over illustrated catalogues while he weighed the merits of various weapons and compared their cost.

Although I was always popping in and out of his house and as 'boy Karl' was on familiar terms with most of his brothers and sisters, Gordon was strangely shy about coming up to the Rectory. When I taxed him with it he just grinned and said: 'I dussent, Karl.'

'Why not?' I insisted. 'I come to your house, don't I?'

He grinned again. 'That 'uden't do, Karl. Your mam 'ud be riled.'

'No she wouldn't. Come on. Come and see my train.'

But he just shook his head and would not be persuaded. It was my first intimation that Betty's reputation was spreading beyond the Old Rectory.

Undoubtedly one of the people who was responsible for this was a white-haired old widow called 'Granny' Burlingham. Originally Granny had been taken on to help with the washing once a week. Then, when our various maids and cooks could no longer stand the pressure and left, she came in and helped out. My father was very much taken with her and there was certainly an indomitable, earthy quality about Granny that was not unattractive, particularly to a Marxist. She might well have found a niche for herself in one of Maxim Gorky's works. I remember the extraordinarily soft skin on her hands and arms and how the backs of her hands were blotched with huge freckles. But she was also two-faced and a gossip, and I didn't trust her at all. She used to sit upstairs with Betty when the baby was being nursed and I would overhear her egging Betty on to tell her things which, for my father's sake, had far better been left untold. When Betty obliged Granny would gasp: 'Why, that he *never*!' and cackle with wicked laughter. She was also fond of telling me that 'little pitchers had long ears'. When I retorted: 'And old 'uns have too!' she took offence and reported me to Betty for being cheeky.

Nevertheless she did not stay with us for very long. She soon discovered the truth of one of her own favourite maxims—'Him as sups with the devil needs a long spoon.' Betty fell out with her, accused her of helping herself from our kitchen garden, and from then on she became 'that old rogue, Granny'. But she never quite dropped out of our lives altogether, and eventually succeeded in ingratiating herself with me by inviting me down to her tiny cottage on the edge of the fen. There in a living room crowded with cuckoo clocks and stuffed humming birds under glass domes she indulged my taste for the forbidden fruit of *Comic Cuts* and *The Funny Wonder*—the only reading matter which interested her eighteen year old step-son Freddie—while she did her level best to pump me about the goings on up at the Old Rectory. I rather enjoyed being questioned because it made me feel important. However, I doubt whether she learnt much from me.

The truth is that what Granny must have picked up in the six or so months she was working for us would have lasted her for the rest of her life without any help from me. Betty realized instinctively that one of the most effective ways of wounding my father was to shame him in public, consequently any sort of gathering of his friends at the Old Rectory was an almost infallible prelude to a row of primeval intensity. Once things were down on all fours she no longer felt herself to be at an intellectual disadvantage. If she finally managed to goad my father into hitting her then her triumph was complete. So, unfortunately, was his own sense of degradation. My own private conviction was that it would have helped matters considerably if he had done it harder and more often. In this, as in most things, my opinion was not called for.

I suspect now that what Betty was warring against was a deeply ingrained sense of her own inferiority. In a very real way my father must have personified for her all that was for ever beyond her reach. The very things he praised so warmly in her—her cooking (which was truly excellent); her management of the household; even the charms of her own body—she persistently undervalued. No doubt when agreeing to marry him, she had hoped that she would somehow come to acquire an equal share in his mind, and she was grievously disappointed. Her sole criterion for success was total possession, and the one part of him which she was never able to possess was the very part which made him into what he was. With each attack he withdrew a little further into himself, became a little more remote from her, a little more 'spiritual'. How galling it must have been for her when, shortly after his arrival at Larling, he discovered a soul-brother literally on the doorstep in the shape of the man who delivered the paraffin—A. W. Votier, who had just finished reading my father's book *God—A Study in Metabiology* for the seventh time. In Betty's view it was just permissible for a dyed-in-the-wool aristocrat like Sir Richard Rees to share my father's eccentric beliefs, but a *paraffin man*!—and a revolutionary socialist one to boot!—that must have been a bitter mouthful for her to swallow.

If only there had been some way in which she could have come to terms with my father's spiritual side all might have been well, but she, in her own way, was as constitutionally incapable of compromise as he was in his. For him this travesty of a marriage was at least as authentic a "life-experience" as either of his others had been, therefore who could say that it might not prove to be "the means to a rare spiritual achievement"? That he could even *conceive* it in such terms demarcates with an awful finality the bottomless gulf that separated them.

9 IN June 1932 Jimmy Young bought himself a house at Rockland St Peter, a village some seven miles north of Larling. Thither he brought his recently acquired American wife Helen and her two daughters by previous marriages, Barbara and Virginia. Within a matter of months the *Sturm und Drang* of life at the Old Rectory of Rockland St Peter was threatening to vie with—and even, on occasion, to surpass—that at the Old Rectory, Larling.

The Youngs visited us frequently and Weg and I struck up a friendship with their younger girl Barbara who was about our own age. She wore a scarlet ribbon in her dark hair which, for a brief period, I found attractive. However, when Barbara responded by forming an attachment to me and following me around everywhere I became exasperated with her and finally lassoed her with a clothes line, trussed her up and left her lying in the meadow. As a way of coping with a troublesome man/woman relation it now strikes me as having certain merits, but it only got me into trouble. I somehow managed to lie myself out of it only to find myself constrained to 'kiss and be friends' which I did with such bad grace that Barbara promptly burst into tears again.

Virginia, the other daughter, was several years older than her half-sister. She was blonde and spoke with an American accent which intrigued me. The difference in our ages did not prevent her from initiating me into the mystery of how babies were conceived—a piece of information which she had recently acquired from her mother who was a doctor. The locale chosen for my initiation was 'Lumley's barn' which formed part of the Rectory outbuildings. Thither Virginia led me, whispering that she had a great secret to impart. And there, lying on her back on the golden straw, she imparted it.

She must have thought me exceptionally obtuse for finally in exasperation she said: 'Well, undo your buttons, you coot, and I'll *show* you!'

Obediently I complied while she swiftly divested herself of her knickers. 'You put *that* in *there*,' she said. 'Now do you get it?'

I peered down at myself and then at the soft golden down which was just beginning to burgeon upon her. The operation she was describing seemed not so much improbable as well nigh impossible—roughly on a par with threading an embroidery needle with a piece of chewed string. 'Are you *sure*, Ginny?' I asked doubtfully.

'Yeah. Mom says the man's penis goes stiff so's he can do it. But I guess you're too young.' She yawned and wriggled back into her drawers. I buttoned myself up again. 'Now don't you go telling anyone I told you,' she cautioned me. 'Cross your heart.'

'What?'

'Say: "Cross my heart and hope to die if I tell".'

I did so, but I still wasn't sure whether I believed her or not.

Other frequent visitors at this time were a family called the Deiners. I believe my father had met them through the Independent Labour Party—James Maxton's old I.L.P.—with which he was now becoming increasingly involved. Stanley and May Deiner lived in Liverpool and had an only daughter called Daphne who was about two years older than I was. She had long, Alice-in-Wonderland hair, a silvery tooth-brace, and tended to give herself airs. She also complained that I was too rough. She and Weg took to giggling in corners and having secrets. This irked me exceedingly though I affected to despise them for it. When we all went bathing in a nearby lake Daphne made a wholly unnecessary palaver about getting undressed without letting me see. Even at that age I think I had the wit to realize that she was a 'tease', hinting at some deliciously wicked female mystery. Since I refused to believe that she was constructed any differently from Virginia or my sisters, my response may well have disappointed her.

Daphne's mother, May, was a petite woman with a pointed nose and short, dark wavy hair. She got on my wrong side right from the start. Her first words to me were: 'I know we're going to be *great* friends'—the kind of approach which always put me on the defensive. She also used bright red nail varnish and lipstick to match, which offended my sense of decorum. I preferred my women unpainted. May appeared undeterred by my coolness and seemed to assume that there was some secret understanding between us. She took to giving me enigmatic little smiles and nods which I found wholly baffling. After about a week of this she cornered me in the walled garden one day and asked me point-blank why I didn't like her. I protested vehemently that I did—quite.

'I always wanted a little boy like you,' she sighed.

This struck me as so grossly improbable that I enquired curiously: 'What's wrong with Daphne? She's yours, isn't she?'

May smiled. 'Daphne's her father's daughter.'

I nodded. I knew exactly what she was getting at. 'Like Weg, you mean?'

She gave me yet another of her thoughtful, enigmatic looks and changed the subject.

May soon chummed up with Betty which was wise on her part but served to increase my distrust of her. Together they talked dressmaking, housekeeping and babies. They also discussed the Youngs. It soon became evident that Betty had taken against Helen Young whom she described as 'two-faced'. It was by eavesdropping on her conversations with May that I learnt that life at the Old Rectory, Rockland St Peter, was every bit as tempestuous as our own. I also learnt a new word 'miscarriage' which, in its context, I found completely mystifying. I filed the information away until I could find someone to elucidate it for me.

For a time it looked as though we might escape a full-blown row while the Deiners were with us because May acted as a sort of safety valve to relieve Betty's emotional pressure. It could not last. Jimmy Young and Helen drove over from Rockland one day and stayed to lunch with us. During the meal Betty sulked. Her long upper lip grew longer and longer and a black cloud seemed to settle over her end of the table. I recognized the warning signs immediately but the Youngs, the Deiners and my father were too engrossed in their conversation to notice them. As soon as lunch was over we children scooted for the sanctuary of the croquet lawn while the adults retired to the drawing room for coffee.

It was not long before I heard Betty's voice. She seemed to wind herself up like an old-fashioned gramophone—a nagging, nasal whine, rising higher and higher, punctuated at irregular intervals by the word 'darlin' '. This indicated to me that it was my father who was in the firing line. Whenever she was gunning for him she always addressed him thus in a sort of parody of endearment which must have set his teeth on edge. I felt the old, familiar sinking feeling in the pit of my stomach and wondered how it would end. As far as I could make out Betty had the floor to herself though I did hear my father say: 'Oh, *do* shut up,' with a note of weary pleading in his voice that was as familiar as it was ineffectual. Betty's whining tirade grew ever more shrill and impassioned and I caught Helen's name. Suddenly, in mid-flow, she cut off. There was no crash of crockery being flung; no demented shrieking; no door crashing shut. With ears pricked I crept up to the open drawing room window and heard Jimmy Young saying in quiet, almost conversational tones: '. . . and if you don't shut your foul mouth woman—and *keep it shut*!—I swear to God that I'll break this log over your bloody, stupid, ignorant head!'

The effect was almost magical. There was a moment of stunned silence, then I heard footsteps and the sound of the drawing room door opening and closing. A few seconds later May's tremulous voice announced: 'I'll go and talk to her, John,' and I heard Jimmy enquiring calmly whether there was any more coffee in the pot.

I risked a quick peep. Stanley Deiner was sitting clasping his knees, looking dazedly down at the carpet. My father was abstractedly tapping his thumbnail with a cigarette preparatory to putting it between his lips. Helen Young was pouring an amber stream of coffee into the cup Jimmy held out to her. I daresay that the reason I remember the scene so clearly is because it was one of the very few occasions in my life when I saw Betty actually brought down in mid-flight.

In a very real sense it is Betty I have to thank for the fact that

I became a thorough-going pantheist without realizing it. When, years later, I came across the line in *Tintern Abbey*: 'Nature then to me was All in All,' I knew at once what Wordsworth meant. I recognized myself. In the Larling woods, on the heaths, among the fields and fens, I found peace. And something more than peace. I found an element, a spirit, that was not indifferent to me; did not reject me. It was my secret pleasure to creep along the overgrown tracks, ghosting between the bushes, moving so silently that more than once I was able to steal up within an arm's length of a nibbling rabbit. I watched the birds like a spy until I found their hidden nests, but felt no urge to take the eggs. What I collected was private knowledge—incidents and places that were known to myself alone—yet all the while I was conscious of that incommunicable sense of having been there before, of re-discovering things already known.

Such loneliness as I knew I carried with me from the house and left among the hedgerows. Out of doors, beneath those limitless Norfolk skies, I needed no one, became a part of what I was among. Even when unhappiness seemed all but insupportable and the tears just would not stop there always came a time when my attention was drawn outside myself to some small wonder of the world without. Thus I remember once trailing half blind across the heath and suddenly hearing an extraordinary *chicker-chicker* which checked the sobs in my throat. I tiptoed forward and peering over the top of the bracken saw two weasels, both poised erect on their hind legs, confronting one another across an arena of cropped grass. They took no notice of me at all, not even when like some left-over wave, a huge, shuddering sigh broke upon my lips. Suddenly one of the creatures leapt—an arching flicker of reddish-brown; a flash of white against the pale green croziers of the young bracken. I heard a piercing squeal and then silence. I pushed forward and found only a tiny tuft of white fur to mark the scene of the drama. I picked it up, brushed it against my lips, and shivered violently.

By the time I reached the age of seven there was hardly a

bird or animal I could not recognize. At that time my eyesight was extraordinarily sharp and sometimes I used to amuse myself by lying on my back in the woods and, staring upwards, picking out a single leaf on the topmost twig of a tall tree. Then, quite how I did it I really don't know, I would isolate and magnify that leaf until I could make out the main and lateral veins on its underside. It was almost as though I had discovered a way of raising myself towards it and so lessening the distance which separated us. I did not think this ability of mine was in any way remarkable. No doubt I assumed that everyone could do the same if they wished, like aiming stones.

My constant disparagement of my own odd talents was to a large extent the result of my growing conviction that I had been born stupid. Whereas Betty was never weary of telling Weg that she was 'lazy and ugly' (both manifestly untrue), in my case it was 'lazy and stupid'. To me there seemed to be plenty of justification for such an assessment of my character. For one thing I was pretty well hopeless at sums. To some extent I got round this at school by copying my answers from George Copsey who was very bright and was eventually to win a coveted scholarship to the local grammar school. I knew that by doing this I was merely postponing the day of reckoning, but living as I did from one day to the next it was not difficult to persuade myself that Armageddon would probably never arrive. Besides, I was good at reading and my raffia mats and plasticene farm animals were at least the equal of the best the Little Room could produce. If only my addition and subtraction had been on a par with my raffia mats what a wonder I might have been! Even so I was utterly astounded when at the end of my third and final term in the Little Room I was handed *The Boy's Wonder Book of Ships* and found inscribed within it in Miss Parrot's best copperplate: *2nd Prize, Standard 4, Awarded to Col Murry.* 2nd Prize for what? I dared not ask. Gordon's opinion was that it was probably for Regular Attendance. It seemed more than likely.

10

THAT summer the procession of our temporary domestics was brought to a timely halt. I arrived home from school one afternoon to find an older sister of Gordon's in the kitchen. Like all the Batleys she was minute—certainly not more than four foot eight—and although I had not met her before I knew I couldn't be mistaken about her lineage. She had a round, chubby face; short, dark, wiry hair, and bandy legs. 'Hello,' I said. 'Who're you?'

'I'm Ruby—Gordon's sister. You're boy Karl, aren't you?'

I admitted it. 'Does *she* know you're here?' I asked.

'I'm the new maid.'

'Go on! Really?'

She nodded, flushing scarlet.

A thought struck me. 'Hey!' I exclaimed. 'Now Gordon'll be allowed up, won't he?'

'I don't know nothing about that.'

'Are you living in?'

She nodded.

'What're you doing now?'

'What's it look like? Getting your Mum and Dad's tea ready.'

I eyed the tray she had prepared and grinned broadly. She had set out the knives and spoons from the kitchen drawer.

'*They* don't have *those*,' I said scornfully.

'Well, you might show us then,' she flashed, 'stead of standing there sniggling!'

So I showed her where the proper tea things were kept and helped her to set the tray. I expected she would last about a fortnight. In fact Rue stayed with us all of nine years. Together with Bodge she came to form part of the permanent fabric of the household and, recognizing her quality, Weg and I made haste to better Polonius' advice and grappled her to our hearts with hoops of love far stronger than any steel.

There was something about Rue that can only be described as indestructible. She was like one of those small, solid rubber balls which however hard you throw it always seems to bounce back even harder. Nothing, not even Betty, could keep her down for long. Her zest for life was in direct counter-proportion to her size. She comforted us and we in our turn consoled her. To sustain her she had a seemingly inexhaustible fund of proverbial catch-phrases. No cloud, for Rue, was without its silver lining; no lane so long that it had no turning. And somewhere along her path through life she had acquired a repertoire of moral narrative verses which we found utterly enthralling. 'Go on, Rue,' we'd urge her. 'Give us the custard one.' And if she was in the right mood she'd fold her plump little hands in her lap, lower her voice to a dramatic throb and recite the tale of Mary who crept into the pantry, scoffed a bowl of custard and, when accused by her mother, tried to blame it on the cat. Since this was just such a ploy as I might have tried in similar circumstances I was with Mary all the way. Alas, of that moral masterpiece nothing now remains to sustain me except the tremendous, clinching climax when Mary's mother cries triumphantly:

A spoon *was in the custard!*
No cat could use a spoon!

There was another long one about a boy who tried to restrain his tearaway companions from throwing mud at a poster of 'Our Saviour', but though this too was in its own way very impressive, for me it did not have quite the charm of the custard saga. I found it difficult to identify with the rather priggish hero, whereas I was with 'wicked Mary' one hundred per cent. But I responded warmly when, over the washing-up, Rue would lead us in a rousing chorus of *Dare to be a Daniel.*

Dare to be a Daniel,
Dare to stand alone,
Dare to pass the public house
And take your money home!

Part of the pleasure here undoubtedly derived from the fact that you could bawl out the third line as 'Dare to pass the public arse' and then look supremely innocent when Rue affected to be shocked.

Her sense of fun was as infectious as it was irrepressible and she had a laugh which sounded exactly like a hen's cackle of triumph at having laid a double-yolked egg. Later on, when Weg and I took to writing plays and staging them in the box-room, Rue was always roped in to take a part. In one—*Septimus's Revenge*—she had to be, among other things, a gipsy fortune-teller squatting in a cave constructed out of a clothes horse draped with blankets. During the performance the cave suddenly subsided on top of her and from under the heaving blankets came Rue's wild crowing laugh. It proved so infectious that not only the rest of the cast but the audience too were reduced to helpless hysteria.

She subscribed to a weekly publication called *The Family Journal*. Since Weg and I were forbidden comics we read Rue's *Journal* from cover to cover, devouring the serials avidly. One—*Diamonds in the Rough*—ran for months, and we argued and debated each twist and turn of its incredibly involved plot. There was a *Letters to the Editor* feature and also a jokes section. Every week a five-shilling postal order was awarded to the reader who sent in the best original joke. Rue decided that this was money for jam but it proved less easy than she had supposed. For days after she had decided to enter she could be observed trotting round the house, an abstracted frown furrowing her forehead and her lips moving silently as if in prayer. Finally she surfaced with what we came to know as 'Rue's joke'. She procured herself a postcard, sat herself down at the kitchen table one evening and, with the tip of her tongue following the laborious track of her nib, transcribed the following:

Judge: Prisoner at the bar, what have you to say for yourself?
Prisoner: A pint of beer, m'lud.

Weg and I read it and glanced at each other. Somehow it seemed to lack a certain something. In fact, as jokes went, it seemed about the feeblest we'd ever heard, and even after Rue had pointed out the subtle play-upon-words in 'bar', we were still dubious. But Rue read it aloud yet again and broke into a delighted cackle. 'When I win,' she said, 'I'll bike straight into Harling and buy us all six pennorth of chips.' She didn't win but we got the chips anyway.

That summer, about a month after Rue came to work for us, we all went off to the seaside on holiday. My father had rented a bungalow for a fortnight in the tiny hamlet of Eccles on the Norfolk coast between Cromer and Yarmouth. Sir Richard Rees also came along. As physical opposites it would be hard to imagine a greater contrast than Rue and Sir Richard. He wavered aloft like a bony totem pole whereas she barely came up to the middle button of his waistcoat. He was the third member of that triumvirate of my father's life-long friends, the other two members being Max Plowman and Jimmy Young. Sir Richard was a shy and extremely gentle person who, thanks no doubt to an ironic sense of humour and a training in the Diplomatic Service, seemed somehow able to cope with Betty's tantrums. Since he was one of the very few people who had approved of my father's marriage to her he may well have felt that he had a vested interest in the matter.

My little step-sister Mary was by now walking and talking. Already she was very much the apple of my father's eye. Both Weg and I were also extremely taken with her, but we were soon given to understand by Betty that Mary belonged to an entirely different class of being from our own. Thus Mary was privileged to use the front stairs at the Old Rectory whereas we were rigorously confined to the back; Mary could leave food on her plate with impunity while we had to masticate gristle till our stomachs heaved; while over and over again it was dinned into us that Mary was both clever and beautiful whereas we were stupid and ugly. In fact Mary was a sweet little girl with enormous grey eyes and a pudding-bowl haircut who followed us round like an adoring puppy and, rather like a puppy, we trained her to wheedle Betty for things we dared not risk asking for ourselves. In the breathless

Above left:
Katherine Mansfield, 1912

Above: Violet, 1922

Left:
John Middleton Murry, 1918

Old Coastguard Station, Abbotsbury

Weg and Col at Abbotsbury

sort of verbal shorthand whereby Ruby had become 'Rue', so Mary became 'Mare'. Betty alone remained 'Betty', though on occasion I bought myself a swift clout across the head by calling her 'Ma'.

No sooner had we arrived at Eccles than Weg, Rue and I overdid the sunbathing and got badly burnt. Our skin bubbled up into vast painful blisters so that we looked as though we were suffering from some nauseating tropical disease. We had competitions to see who could peel off the longest unbroken strip and played interminable games of Ludo. The three of us slept in a bell tent up and down which, much to Rue's dismay, little brown lizards scuttled in the hot sunshine. One morning, in a fury, Betty flung a cup of hot cocoa at my father. It missed him but hit the wall of the bungalow with a resounding crash and left it looking like an abattoir. On the whole it was a pretty good holiday. None of us cried much.

It was in this year that we acquired some new friends. These were the de Jongs—'Steppie' and Piet. Piet was a professional archaeologist who spent half of each year at the site of the Palace of Knossos in Crete where he was in charge of the museum. He was also a skilled architectural draughtsman and model engineer. The de Jongs' cottage in the nearby village of Snetterton was a strange and delightful place. It had its own peculiar smell—a sort of heavy, heady mixture of Turkish tobacco, incense and garlic—and the walls of the sitting room were lined with row upon row of Piet's meticulously drawn and coloured cartoons of all his archaeologist friends. Piet was lean and brown. He wore a rakish blue beret and sped around in a scarlet M.G. sports car. Steppie drove a small, sedate saloon, sported a series of remarkable straw hats and was by no means lean. She went in for hand-knitted jumpers, jangly bangles, and long rattling strings of wooden beads. Her face with its wide, mobile mouth put one irresistibly in mind of a large and amicable frog.

The de Jongs had no children of their own which was a pity because Piet would have made a marvellous father for any boy. He showed me how to construct kites and model gliders and took us fishing with bread and bent pins in the nearby stream. He also talked to me as if I were a grown-up and was intrigued by my ability to hit things with stones. One day he took me out into his garden where he had set up a tin can on the end of a bamboo cane. He paced out a series of marks, pushed a peg into the lawn at each one and laid out five pebbles beside each peg. Then he sat down with a pencil and scribbling pad and told me to fire away. I was delighted at an opportunity to show off. I soon 'found the line' and, one after another, the pebbles rattled against the can. I tried to explain to him how I did it, but since I didn't really know myself, I don't suppose he was able to make much of it. For my part I was only too happy to be the centre of attention.

I once stayed with the de Jongs for a few days. Steppie introduced me to *omelettes aux fines herbes*, which she made superbly, and also to *The Story of Babar the Elephant*. One of Jean de Brunhoff's illustrations showed Babar tormented by monstrous nightmares. I laughed heartily at it. But that night I woke in an absolute sweat of terror pursued by the sort of horrible phantoms that might have been extruded from the studio of Heironymous Bosch. I lay, rigid with terror, and yelled at the top of my voice. Steppie appeared in a sprigged cotton nightie, bearing a candle. 'What is it?' she said, bending over me. 'What's the matter?'

'The things,' I chattered. 'The things were after me.'

'What things, my pet?'

What things? I did not know, nor did I care to know. I reached out and clung to that large and friendly bosom as though it were a life raft. She set down her candlestick on the chest of drawers, climbed into bed beside me and held me tight until I slept.

The de Jongs were to remain friends of ours for several years, partly, I'm sure, because they spent a good deal of their lives abroad and Betty was therefore prevented from building up a real head of steam against them. She managed it finally, of course, but that was still far into the future. Meanwhile she had her work cut out disposing of a number of singular characters who, I suspect, were drawn to the Old Rectory by rumoured reports that my father was the new Messiah. Such visitors were indeed privileged to witness his almost daily crucifixion, but it can hardly have been what they had in mind.

My sister and I took these exotic migrants as we found them. To those who were prepared to acknowledge our existence we responded warmly. Most delightful by far was an old Irish Buddhist with a snowy white beard and twinkling blue eyes called Mr Loutet. He was exactly like a character out of one of the fairy tales to which I had by then become addicted and he had one especial talent which seemed to us wholly magical—he was a skilled ventriloquist. We would be sitting with him in the drawing room when a squeaky little voice would pipe up from behind the sofa: 'I wish someone would let me out! Oh, I *do* wish someone would let me out!' Weg and I would stare at one another wide-eyed in astonishment. Then we would turn to Mr Loutet who, as like as not, would be reading a book and paying no attention to us. 'Did you hear that, Mr Loutet?' we'd ask.

'Eh?' he'd murmur, blinking up at us guilelessly. 'What was that, my dears?'

'A little voice,' we'd say. 'It seemed to be behind the sofa.'

He would then cock his head on one side, touch his fingers to his ear, appear to listen hard, and then shake his head. 'I can't hear anything.'

'*Please* let me out!'

'There!' we'd cry. 'You *must* have heard it that time!'

'Oh, that was just a bird outside the window.'

'No, no. It was someone saying: "Let me out!"'

And so it would go on until he had us hunting all round the room trying to find this mysterious little character who was beseeching our help.

Sometimes he would tell us stories—marvellous tales of princes and princesses, of winged horses and jewelled, flame-snorting dragons who lived in strange countries under the ground where the sky was made up of woven tree-roots—

while we sat there, goggle-eyed, completely spellbound. Alas for poor, gentle Mr Loutet. Betty flew at him one day and accused him of enticing us into the drawing room after she had expressly forbidden us to set foot in there. He was swirled out of the house like a dead leaf before a tempest and we never saw him again.

Then there was a wild and rather scary little Scotswoman who used to descend upon us at irregular intervals and hold long conversations alone in her bedroom with John the Baptist and the Archangel Gabriel. She was kind enough to us in her odd way but we were inclined to agree with Betty's assessment of her that she was barmy. One day I hid myself in the lilac bushes and peeped out at her as she strolled in the paddock. Every now and again she would curtsy profoundly to left or right and, as I watched her, I too began to imagine that there *were* real people around her whom she could see and I couldn't. Then, to my utter dismay, she suddenly pivoted round, her green tartan cape flaring outwards, and pointed her finger precisely at where I was concealed. 'Aha, wee curious eyes!' she called, 'I know fu' well ye're there!' I held my breath in fear but she only chuckled and wandered off along the cow track. I never followed her again.

Another odd character, but one who fell into a somewhat different category, was 'Old Jimmy'. He was what is known technically as an 'old lag' and about twice a year he used to turn up at the Old Rectory pushing a broken down pram. He would then take up his quarters in the toolshed. Though she grumbled about him, Betty never went for Old Jimmy in the way she did for the others and she usually sent us down the yard with a plate of dinner for him. We left it on the granary steps, banged on the toolshed door and yelled, 'Dinner, Jimmy!' before scampering away. He was excessively secretive and made a practice of stuffing the toolshed keyhole with newspaper to prevent our peeping in. After he departed he always left an odd, sweetish smell lingering behind him. One day I asked Bodge what it was. 'Meths,' he said.

These people remain far more vivid in my memory than any

of the various literary celebrities to whom we were occasionally introduced. Not that there were many of these since, at about this time, my father's specifically literary reputation was approaching its nadir. He himself did not seem unduly perturbed about this and thus it came as a considerable surprise to us when he suddenly went off the deep end about some woman called Catherine Carswell. She, it appeared, had written a book about D. H. Lawrence in which she had scattered around libels about my father as though she were spreading dung. For the first time in my life I saw my father really angry. 'Poisonous bitch,' he fumed. 'Is there to be no end to this sort of libellous filth?' And for once he actually did something about it. The book was withdrawn from circulation and a public apology was made, but I doubt if it did any good really. My father had got himself cast in the stock rôle of villain in the Lawrence Saga and it was to be many years and many, many more books before Richard Aldington and Harry Moore eventually started to put the record straight. By then my father was long past caring.

It was just after the Carswell episode that Frieda Lawrence came to stay for a weekend. My father had spoken up for her in a law case about Lawrence's missing will which he had witnessed in 1914. Frieda won the case and, partly as a result, effected a reconciliation after the breach caused by *Son of Woman*, my father's critical study of Lawrence. I remember Frieda only as a rather large, smiley woman who invited Weg and me to go and stay with her on her ranch in New Mexico. 'Would we have to go to school?' I enquired carefully. She shook with laughter. 'No, no,' she said. 'No more school.' It seemed an excellent proposition to me and I was sorry that my father did not take her up on it. Her visit ended in a vintage row in which Betty smashed a Dresden candlestick. Frieda must have felt it was quite like the old times in Zennor.

II

BACK at school once more I now found myself in the Big Room. This was presided over by Mrs Hewetson, the wife of a friendly poultry farmer whose territory, patrolled by fierce dogs, abutted ours on the southern side. Mrs Hewetson was a quiet-voiced woman who, nevertheless, seemed to have no difficulty in controlling her large class. She informed me, quietly, that she was expecting great things of me. She must have been very disappointed when, at the end of the spring term, I emerged bottom of the whole class—26th out of 26! Considering the competition for this honour it must have taken some doing. My father, thinking back to his own prodigious school days, commented wryly in his journal "The contrast is amusing. I was top of the ex-7th standard in a Higher Grade Board school at 7; Col, at the same age, is bottom of a village school." True enough, but at the age of 44 he still couldn't tell the difference between a thrush and a hen blackbird.

Looking back on it I find it difficult to decide just why I was quite so bad. In spite of Betty's unceasing assertions to the contrary I was really rather a bright little boy. Even my father acknowledged this grudgingly from time to time. I suppose a lot of it was to do with whether my interest was engaged, and Mrs Hewetson, for all her excellent qualities, somehow never succeeded in engaging it. I spent most of my time daydreaming. The only lessons I enjoyed at all were reading and drawing. I shared a desk with a white-haired boy called Ernie Stebbings who was two years older than I was and could draw quite beautifully. His family were very hard up and he knew he would have to leave school at fourteen and go out to work. In the meantime he seemed determined to cram a lifetime's drawing into five short years.

My Uncle Richard had given me a small Windsor & Newton watercolour box for my birthday. I took it with me to school and showed it to Ernie. His pale cheeks went even paler when he saw it. 'Go on,' I said. 'You can use it too.'

'Honest, boy Karl?'

I nodded.

He went and got a jam jar of clean water, set it down on the desk before him, took out a pencil sketch of a yellowhammer perched on a thorn twig and began to colour it. I watched him enthralled, but I don't think he was aware of me at all. He was in a world of his own—totally absorbed in creating something beautiful. He drew entirely from memory and, as far as birds were concerned, he must have had what amounted to eidetic recall for his detail was invariably perfect. One sketch he did I remember above all the rest. It was a study of a moorhen thrusting its timid way out between the reeds at the river's edge. I swear you could almost hear the creature cluck.

The only lesson I remember from my time in the Big Room was not really a lesson at all but a temperance lecture. A little fat man with pale, bulging blue eyes appeared before us one afternoon and Mrs Hewetson told us all to sit up straight and pay attention. I thus learnt for the first time about 'the Demon Drink'. There was the Beer Demon who was pretty awful and could paralyse you at a stroke, but he was as docile as a spring lamb compared to the Strong Spirit. To demonstrate just how powerful *he* was, the little man produced a tin saucer and poured into it the merest teaspoonful of some mysterious colourless liquid. He then struck a match and touched the saucer. A beautiful, orange-tipped, purply-blue flame wavered in the air like a butterfly's wing. 'You see!' he cried triumphantly. 'Imagine that flaming and gnawing at your vitals! Whisky and gin, my young friends! Try thinking of it as poison!'

'Ah, tha's meths, that is,' murmured a sceptical voice from the back of the class.

Mrs Hewetson frowned and shook her head. The lecturer took out his handkerchief and mopped his glistening brow. Then he invited us all to step up and sign The Pledge. Sheepishly we did so, queueing up before Mrs Hewetson's desk.

My father was highly amused when I told him about it, especially when I informed him that, since no mention had been made of wine, his own vitals were, presumably, still safe.

It must have been at about this time that my father decided Weg ought to learn to play the piano. Since we did not possess a piano one was to be purchased for her. She would have piano lessons at Norwich High School for Girls which she would be joining as a boarder at the beginning of the summer term. Weg, I thought, looked a little apprehensive but, on the whole, pleased. My father turned to me. 'And how about you, old boy? What would you like?'

If he had been expecting me to ask for a violin he was disappointed. I knew exactly what I wanted. 'A dog,' I said.

My father blinked. 'A dog?'

Betty said: 'You don't want a dog. Nasty smelly things.'

'I *do*,' I insisted. 'Please let me. *Please!*'

My father smiled. 'All right, old boy, so you shall. What sort would you like?'

Wild with delight I raced upstairs to the nursery, dragged out an illustrated story book and found the picture I was looking for; a line drawing of a ragged but friendly looking mongrel with a black patch all but obscuring one eye. I hastened back downstairs and showed it to him. 'One like that,' I said.

My father pushed his glasses up on to his forehead and examined the picture. 'Yes, that looks a very sensible sort of dog,' he said. 'What will you call him?'

'Scotty,' I said firmly.

'But he isn't a scottie, you know.'

'That's just his *name*,' I said. 'Not what he *is*. Max Plowman isn't a ploughman, is he?'

My father conceded the point and I went off happily to tell Bodge and Rue.

Weg's piano duly appeared. A handsome upright instrument with gleaming brasswork, the strange name *Bosendorfer* inlaid upon it, and interesting maroon felt pads where the foot pedals joined the frame. We were forbidden to touch it. Since no one in the family could play we had to wait till Steppie appeared before we actually heard it. Then we gathered round while she played selections from *The Daily Express Community*

Song Book and we joined in the singing. I enjoyed it enormously and in next to no time had the tunes and words of a dozen songs off by heart. When one evening my father said: 'You know, old Col sings better than any of us,' I felt as if I had been knighted on the spot.

As the time approached for Weg's departure I gently raised the subject of my dog again. 'We'll have to see about it when you get back from Brighton,' said my father.

'Brighton?' It was the first I'd heard of it. 'What about Brighton?'

'Oh, didn't I tell you? You're going to stay with Grandpa.'

'For how long?'

'A month or two.'

'By myself?'

'That's right.'

'Do I *have* to?'

He smiled reassuringly. 'It's all fixed up, old boy. You'll enjoy it.'

All fixed up? I'd enjoy it? Would I? I wondered. Still there would always be Scotty to look forward to when I got back.

12

ON April 16th, 1934 my father took me up to London by train and handed me over to his father under the clock at Victoria Station. It was the first time I had seen the old man since Weg and I had been parked with him while my father and Betty were looking for Larling. On that occasion he had expressed his attitude towards disobedient small boys in general and myself in particular by booting me up the front steps of the dark little terrace house he owned in Dawson Terrace, off Freshfield Road below the racecourse. It had been a salutary and painful experience. Quite frankly I found him terrifying.

Grandpa had a thick, yellowish, 'Kitchener' moustache, a

heavy jowl, and broad, hairy hands. Across his waistcoat was looped a silver chain at the end of which was fastened a silver fob watch. As my father and I approached him at Victoria he pulled this instrument out, stared at it accusingly, sniffed loudly and said: 'You're late, Jack.' He followed this up immediately with: 'Has the boy passed water?'

My father accompanied us to the train then shook hands with Grandpa and gave me a kiss. 'Cheerio, old boy,' he said.

I watched him stride away up the platform until I lost sight of his grey flannel suit among the crowd. Grandpa had taken off his hard, curly-brimmed hat and placed it on the luggage rack beside my suitcase. He settled back in a corner, unfolded a copy of *The Daily Mail* and started to read. I sat opposite him and watched a brisk, red-legged pigeon skipping between the sleepers on the empty track beside us.

'Grandpa?'

'What is it, boy?'

'Nothing.' It had been on the tip of my tongue to ask him why I was being sent to stay with him. Luckily I thought better of it.

Then, to my astonishment and delight, my father suddenly reappeared. In his hand he held a comic and a bar of Cadbury's Milk Chocolate. He gave them to me and grinned. I was speechless. 'Here,' he said, thrusting his hand into his trousers pocket. 'Don't spend it all at once.' He winked hugely, pushed half-a-crown into my hand, and was gone again. I looked down at the coin, at the copy of *The Rainbow*, at the blue wrapper on the bar of chocolate, and began, very quietly, to cry.

We took a tram from Brighton Station down to The Pavilion and then another along 'The Level' and up Freshfield Road. Three quarters of the way up the hill we got off. The sun was shining brightly and far away over the trembling roofs I glimpsed the distant sea and two tiny steamers crawling up the Channel towards Dover. 'Don't dawdle, boy!' growled Grandpa, stomping on ahead, his walking stick tap-tapping among the dry dog-turds. I hurried after him with my heavy suitcase bumping against my bare knees. We turned past the petrol filling station on the corner and descended the slope of Dawson Terrace.

Grandma was watching out for us from the window of the front parlour and she had the front door open before we reached the steps. 'Hello,' she called. 'Hello, Colin, my dear.'

'Don't fuss over the boy, Mother.'

'But he's tired. It's been a long journey for him.' She stooped over me and kissed me. Her cheek was soft but her chin was hairy. She seemed very old. I relinquished my suitcase gratefully and followed Grandpa up the steps into the house.

4, Dawson Terrace, Brighton was as unlike the Old Rectory, Larling as it is possible to imagine. Downstairs were two poky rooms—the front and back parlour—and a tiny kitchen. The back parlour, which was really the main living room, had a large heavy table, a coal range with a blackleaded oven, and a glass-panelled door which gave access to the garden. The windows were all lace-netted. The garden was tiny and was prinked out with innumerable little gritty paths bordered with scallop shells. As far as I could see Grandpa appeared to grow mainly bamboo canes and string.

Grandma took me up the steep dark stairs and introduced me to my bedroom. It had a white-painted iron bedstead, a washstand with a white earthenware bowl and ewer, and a chest of drawers. On the wall was a small oleograph of *The Light of the World* by Holman Hunt. I looked out of the narrow window and could just make out a sparkling splinter of sea between two distant gasometers. 'Do you like it?' asked Grandma.

'Oh, yes,' I said, 'it's lovely.' But my heart felt heavy.

Downstairs again I was shown the gloomy front parlour. Beside the mantelpiece hung a sepia photograph of my father as a boy, dressed in the extraordinary priestlike uniform of Christ's Hospital. On the floor was a black sheepskin rug. The table was covered by a thick, brocaded green cloth with a beaded fringe. There was an oil lamp with a pink china base and a white shade. The armchairs were covered in shiny imitation leather. In one dark corner was a bookcase with a glass front. Inside it were some copies of my father's books. This dark little house was to be my home for 'a month or two'. Why? I shall never know.

Grandma unpacked my suitcase and laid my clothes neatly in the chest of drawers. I had brought two books with me, Hans Andersen's *Fairy Tales* and *The Myths and Legends of Ancient Greece and Rome*. I had also brought my ancient teddy bear. Grandma looked at him and smiled. 'That's not a bear,' she chuckled, 'it's a threadbare.'

But when I went up to bed that evening my precious bear had disappeared! I couldn't believe my eyes. I hunted all through the bed, in the chest of drawers, and even in the empty ewer. There was no trace of him anywhere. I ran downstairs and burst into the back parlour. 'He's gone!' I wailed. 'Someone's stolen him!'

Grandma looked at my distraught face and turned beseeching eyes upon Grandpa who just sat gazing stolidly ahead into his newspaper. 'Boys don't need dolls,' he growled.

'*You've* taken him!' I gasped. 'Where is he?'

'Say your prayers, my boy, and go to bed.'

'He's *mine*!' I wailed and flung myself weeping upon Grandma.

'Shush now, my pet,' she murmured. 'Shush. You must be a big boy,' and she lifted me up and carried me out of the room.

She took me back upstairs, undressed me and put me into bed. '*Please*, Grandma,' I begged her. '*Please* let me have him back. *Please!*'

She laid her finger to her lips. 'Stop crying then,' she whispered, 'and I'll see what I can do.'

I heard the stairs creak as she went down, then the sound of a door opening and closing. At last I heard her coming back. She walked past my room and along the passage into her and Grandpa's bedroom. Then she came back, opened my door and came in carrying my bear. She brought him over to me and tucked him in beside me. I reached up and hugged her to me.

As her cheek pressed briefly against mine I felt it was wet. At that moment I think I hated my grandfather more than anyone in the whole world.

Next morning at breakfast the prevailing gloom began to lift a little. A postcard had arrived for me from my Aunt Doll, my grandmother's younger sister, who lived in London. She informed me that she would be coming down to Brighton on Saturday and was looking forward to taking me out. In the meantime Grandma was going to get me fitted up with a school blazer because, on the following Monday, I was to start at a new school. Glancing across at Grandpa who was sitting in his shirt sleeves slurping up dark brown tea through his moustache, I began to feel that school might, after all, have unexpected advantages to offer.

True to her word Aunt Doll appeared at ten o'clock on the Saturday morning. She must already have been halfway into her sixties but she still had the heart of a girl of sixteen. Grandpa thoroughly disapproved of her and grumbled that she'd spoil me, but Aunt Doll just winked at me and said: 'Oh, fiddlesticks!' and hustled me out of the house. In no time at all I found I had told her all about my bear. She pursed up her lips and looked thoughtful. Then she said: 'I'll come down to Brighton every Saturday while you're here, dearie, and take you out. And I'll send you two postcards a week. That's a promise. Now let's go on the pier and enjoy ourselves.'

And so another new life-pattern was established. I soon accommodated myself to it. After breakfast Grandma brushed my hair, handed me a penny and I trotted next door where I collected Barbara King, a golden-haired, sausage-curled little girl of my own age. Side by side we made our way down Dawson Terrace, turned the corner past the sweetshop, skirted the iron-railed playing field of Brighton College, and plodded up the hill to Mrs Wilburn's house which had a small black and white notice fastened to its green painted iron gate—Greyfern Infant and Junior School.

Greyfern was run by Mrs Wilburn, a war-widow, and her daughter Beryl. There were about twenty pupils whose ages ranged from six to ten. The school consisted of the first floor of Mrs Wilburn's large Victorian house. There were two main schoolrooms; one which held a piano was for the smaller children, and the other larger one for the juniors. Mrs Wilburn, who had silver-blue hair and played the piano, looked after the little ones; Beryl, who had soft brown hair and grey eyes, looked after us. It was the happiest school I was ever at. In the three months I was there I never once heard a voice raised in anger, and Miss Wilburn had a way of smiling dreamily either at us or out of the window which I found extremely attractive. I learnt that she was to be married in the summer and that the school would then close down.

I spent much of my time drawing maps of the British Isles. I enjoyed this and it also taught me how the various counties and principal towns were distributed; knowledge which I have since found useful on many occasions. I also discovered poetry. Miss Wilburn used to read to us from *Hiawatha* for the last quarter of an hour before school ended. She also read us *The Revenge* by Tennyson and *The Pied Piper of Hamelin* by Robert Browning. I enjoyed them all immensely: so much so, in fact, that one afternoon, after school ended, I overcame my shyness and begged to be allowed to borrow the book she read from and to take it home with me. Miss Wilburn smiled her gentle, abstracted smile and said that I could. The book was called *Stories in Verse* and by that evening I had finished it. When I returned it to her the following morning and told her how much I had enjoyed it she smiled again and asked if I would like to borrow another book. I did so, and thereafter my evenings became almost pleasurable.

One day we were all given a different verse of Tennyson's 'The Brook' to learn for homework. Mine was—

I wind about, and in and out,
With here a blossom sailing
And here and there a lusty trout
And here and there a grayling.

It took me less than a minute to get it by heart and, well inside half an hour, I had memorized the whole poem. I thought it was quite beautiful and, perhaps because it evokes for me the countryside I loved so much, I still do.

Next morning Miss Wilburn called on us to recite it. The first child stumbled through the first two lines of his verse and then dried up. Miss Wilburn smiled tolerantly and asked if anyone could help him. My hand shot up of its own accord. 'Very well, Colin,' she said. 'What do you think comes next?'

Not wanting to waste anything I went back to the beginning:

'I come from haunts of coot and hern,
I make a sudden sally
And sparkle out among the fern,
To bicker down a valley.'

'That's very good,' she said. 'And can you go on?'

Could I not! What a question! I nodded emphatically and was fairly launched. By the time I had reached my own verse you could have heard a pin drop. I imagine the other children were all having bets with themselves as to whether I'd manage it. I did, triumphantly, and Miss Wilburn laid her book down on the table in front of her and laughed and clapped her hands. All the rest of the class joined in, whereupon I promptly ducked down and hid my flaming face inside my desk. Had I but known it I had then reached the absolute apogee of my scholastic career.

On two afternoons a week we all formed up into a crocodile and trudged up a dusty path behind the allotments to the Downs beside the race-course. There we played rounders and, once again, my star shone brightly. An annual Greyfern Sports Cup was awarded for rounders scored, the table for which was headed by a tall, brown-skinned boy called Marcus. He already had two terms' start on me but, by the beginning of June, I had caught him up and passed him. Marcus was distinctly put out by this act of *lèse majesté* and, since he was the

School Captain he had fair reason to be. Miss Wilburn proved equal to the occasion. She let it be known that as the Sports Cup was traditionally awarded for the whole year and I had only been at Greyfern for one term I was not strictly eligible. Instead she was donating a special Progress Prize which I had won. It turned out to be a copy of Palgrave's *Golden Treasury*. I also got the old tennis racquet we used as our 'rounders' bat.

By far the worst day of my week at Brighton was Sunday. For one thing it was the furthest away from Saturday. The heady delights of playing the football slot-machine against Aunt Doll or watching for the umpteenth time as the jerky little clockwork models re-enacted *The Execution of Mary Queen of Scots* were six long days off. The only thing to look forward to on Sundays was the glass of ginger beer which I was allowed after my Sunday afternoon walk.

I took this exercise in the company of Grandpa. Dressed in my navy blue blazer with the brass buttons I trotted along beside him as, with measured tread, he paced the length of the Lower Promenade following the course of Volk's Electric Railway as far as Blackrock. There we turned and retraced our steps. I don't recall our ever going a different way, nor do I remember him conversing with me. Perhaps he saw me as a sort of substitute for a dog. Certainly his growls of caution when we crossed the road were a kind of human equivalent to 'Heel, boy!'

During these dismal patrols I kept up my spirits by thinking of the glass of ginger beer which awaited me when we got home. To intensify the anticipated luxury I strove to make myself even more thirsty by dropping a few steps behind Grandpa and there, concealed from his view, hanging out my tongue and panting fiercely. Unfortunately, while I was thus engaged one hot afternoon, he happened to catch sight of my reflection in a shop window as we were passing. He whirled round, brandishing his walking stick, and accused me of trying to make a damned mockery of him. I did my best to explain what I was up to but this only served to remind him of a way to punish my insolence. I was expressly forbidden all taste of ginger beer from henceforward.

Yet for all his untiring efforts Grandpa never succeeded in cowing me completely. Now and again a mischievous devil would possess me and persuade me to do something quite dreadful just to see what would happen. One such attempt was successful beyond all but my wildest dreams. Every Sunday at lunch Grandpa treated himself to a bottle of stout. This was placed on the table and allowed to settle for half an hour before we ate. One morning I was alone in the back parlour and Grandpa was out in the garden fiddling with his string and his bamboo canes when my eye alighted on the brown bottle. Without pausing to consider the possible consequences I seized hold of it and shook it vigorously.

Five minutes later Grandma and Grandpa took their places at the table. Grandma nodded to me and I intoned dutifully: 'For what we are about to receive may the Lord make us truly thankful.' Grandpa grunted, pushed the corner of his napkin into his collar, and reached out for his bottle. I ducked my head and peered up from under my lowered eyebrows. He gripped the screw stopper and twisted it deftly. There was a loud hiss, a *pop*, and a jetting arc of nicotine-yellow foam fountained right across the table into Grandma's lap; then, as he fought to get the stopper back, Grandpa got his share too. I let out a sort of throttled squeak of nervous excitement, slid off my chair and rushed for a dishcloth. For some extraordinary reason Grandpa did not accuse me of the crime. Perhaps even his sombre imagination could not encompass human enormity on so diabolical a scale.

On another Sunday I was playing with some dominoes on the floor of the front parlour when I discovered a sixpence which had slipped down a crack between two floorboards. I fished it out with a hairpin. I knew I ought to have taken it straight to Grandma but I didn't. Since Grandpa had already taken charge of the half-crown my father had given me, and this was being doled out to me at the rate of a penny a day to buy a glass of milk and a biscuit during school break, I no doubt reasoned it had better be 'finders keepers' if I ever hoped to capitalize on my good fortune.

I did this the very next morning. As Barbara and I passed the little sweetshop on the corner I darted inside and bought four licorice 'bootlaces' and four bars of pink and white nougat all at a ha'penny each, and two sherbert fountains at a penny. Guilt must have prompted me to be generous for I divided my booty scrupulously with Barbara. By the time we reached Greyfern most of it had been consumed, and my appetite for nougat, never very capacious, had been more than satisfied. I wrapped up the remaining half bar in its scrap of greaseproof paper, pushed it into the breast pocket of my blazer, and forgot all about it.

That evening I had just settled down in bed with Hans Andersen when I heard Grandpa call up the stairs: 'Come down here, boy!'

My stomach recognized the tone of his voice and shrank to the size of a peanut. But even so I could not immediately think of anything I had done wrong. I pulled on my slippers, crossed my fingers, and pattered down. I opened the door of the back parlour and peeped in. Grandpa was standing with his legs apart before the range. He was swaying gently backwards and forwards on his heels. Grandma was sitting before the table looking worried. In front of her was my blazer and her needlework basket.

'Come here, boy.'

I relinquished the door knob and edged into the room.

'What's this?'

His right hand, which had been concealed behind his back, now emerged. It was holding that forgotten, half of a chewed bar of bright pink nougat.

'Nougat?' I offered helpfully.

'Where did you get it?'

For a despairing moment I juggled with the notion of saying that Barbara had given it to me. 'At Haskins,' I muttered.

'Speak up.'

'Haskins.'

'And who gave you the money?'

I looked down at the floor.

'Well, boy, I'm waiting.'

'I—I found it,' I whispered miserably.

'Stole it, you mean.'

Did I? I certainly knew what *he* meant!

'So that's the way Jack's brought you up, eh? To be a thief.'

'I didn't steal it,' I whispered, fighting against my tears. 'I found it. Down a crack.'

'It wasn't yours and you took it. That's stealing. Well, now I'm going to teach you what happens to people who steal. Come over here.'

My slippers seemed to have grown lead soles. I shuffled slowly forwards and, as I came within range, he fetched me a clout across the side of the head that made my ear explode. My skull was still ringing when I got a second thump from the other side.

'Now say you're sorry.'

I was sorry all right, though not perhaps in quite the way he imagined.

I daresay my Grandfather had any number of sterling qualities but I must confess I never discovered what they were. The only way I could come to terms with him at all was by thinking of him as something out of my book of Greek legends—the archetypal tyrant. In his small City-state he was the Law and Police Force combined, and the worst crime of all in his civil code was disobedience.

He also had fixed ideas on health. These were very simple and could be summed up in the phrase: 'All illness is imaginary.' If *he* couldn't feel your pain, then you couldn't feel it either. It was a convenient creed in that it saved him unnecessary expense, but it didn't prevent my being driven almost distracted by the toothache. My only recourse when the pain became insufferable was to creep into the front parlour and crawl underneath the black sheepskin hearthrug. There in the dusty uterine darkness I prayed with all my heart that I might die or be spirited away, I cared not where. One evening Grandma found me there curled up asleep and, without telling Grandpa, sneaked me off next morning to a dentist who pulled out the offending tooth. My fear that Grandpa might find out what we had done was almost worse than the pain had been.

It was towards the end of my third and final month at Brighton that I committed the ultimate offence of deliberate disobedience. This too happened on a Sunday. For some reason Grandpa elected to take Grandma with us on our afternoon walk. And not only Grandma. To my surprise and delight, Barbara King was also invited along. All went well until, on the way back, Barbara whispered the suggestion to me that we could run on ahead and get back to Dawson Terrace before my grandparents. There was no question of our getting lost since we both knew the way blindfolded. I don't think I hesitated for a moment but scampered off with her as hard as I could go. I heard Grandpa calling to me to come back but I pretended not to hear. In a moment we were both well out of earshot and were back at the house a full fifteen minutes before Grandpa and Grandma eventually appeared. He came stumping up the pavement towards us with a face that froze my soul. Barbara prudently vanished up the steps into her house and left me to face him alone.

Grandpa's first expression of his displeasure was to swipe me across the shoulders with his walking stick, then he caught hold of me by my collar and the seat of my pants and flung me bodily against the front door. Since it was shut I bounced off and fetched up on the doorstep. He still hadn't actually uttered a word, but his jowls had gone the colour of a turkey's wattles—a sort of dark, purplish red—which was utterly unnerving. Somehow he got the door open, dragged me inside, and began booting me up the passage, grunting 'Damned . . . insolent . . . young . . . puppy!' with each thump of his boot. At the final kick my face met the newel post of the banisters and I clutched it howling with pain and fear. 'Get up to your room!' he choked. 'Up! Up!'

I didn't need telling twice. I was upstairs and inside with the door bolted before his stick was in the umbrella stand. I stayed there for hours, too terrified even to risk going for a pee. As bed time approached Grandma came up and tapped on the door. 'Colin, dear,' she said. 'I think you'd better come down now and say you're sorry.'

But this little worm had finally turned. 'No,' I sobbed. 'I'm going to stay here till Aunt Doll comes and ask her to take me back to London with her.'

'But you shouldn't have disobeyed him, dear. Not with Barbara there. You know how angry it makes him.'

'I hate him!' I sniffed. 'He's a big bully and I *hate* him!'

'Colin, dear, please. For my sake. There's a good boy.'

I fingered my cheek which was still tender, and swollen from its contact with the banisters and from my tears. What was the use? Sister Verity, Betty, Grandpa, it was all one and the same thing. They beat you and broke you and then you had to crawl to them and beg them to forgive you.

'Colin, dear . . . ?'

'All right, Grandma.'

There was no mirror in my bedroom so I had no idea what I looked like. But when I opened the door to let Grandma in the first thing she did was to put her hand up to her mouth, then she caught me in her arms and pressed me to her tenderly. She fetched a cold flannel and wiped my face with it, saying as she did so: 'Oh dear, oh dear.' What had evoked this, I later discovered, was a real peach of a black eye, though, truth to tell, it did not hurt nearly so much as the place where Grandpa's boot had caught me in the middle of the back. I daresay if I'd had my wits about me I could have used my injuries as some sort of blackmail to get him to leave me alone, but I knew from experience that it wouldn't have worked. These things were ordained and there was no escaping them.

When I got downstairs and told Grandpa how sorry I was for having disobeyed him he hardly glanced up from his paper. When he did, and caught sight of my shiner, he just growled, 'What have you done to your eye?'

'I'm sorry,' I mumbled. 'I promise I won't do it again.'

He looked at me with undisguised contempt and gestured me out of the room.

One ironic little postscript has survived my 'holiday' in Brighton. It is a letter I wrote home during my stay. I pencilled it at Grandma's dictation, sitting at the table in the back parlour.

4, Dawson Terrace,
Brighton.

10th June, 1934

Dear Daddy,

I hope you are now home safely and that you all had a nice holiday. I am quite happy and getting along nicely at school. Love to you all.

From your loving son
John.

13

AT the very end of July my Uncle Richard collected me and took me back to Larling. The day before I left Brighton Aunt Doll came down for the last time, bringing with her the gift of a Hornby clockwork motor-boat. We went to the pond in Victoria Park and sailed it together, she on one side of the pond and I on the other. On one trip the motor stalled when the boat was half way across. I stared at it in dismay but Aunt Doll said: 'Oh well, it's not that deep. Take off your socks and shoes and paddle in after it.' I did so and spent the next half hour happily wading around after my boat. 'Better not tell *them* when we get back,' she said, rubbing me down with her hanky. 'Least said's soonest mended.'

Dear Aunt Doll! 'Your dad,' she told me once, 'was never a *real* boy at all. He was just a little old man. And that was *his* doing.' I knew to whom she was referring and, for a brief moment, the imagined horror of having Grandpa for a *father* made me shudder. But I think now that it also helped me to understand why my father hardly ever punished me when I misbehaved. Even so it could not explain why he had condemned me to Brighton in the first place.

When I got back to Larling he asked me how I had enjoyed my stay. I told him all about Aunt Doll and how she had taken me out every Saturday.

'But surely that wasn't *all* you did, was it, old boy?'

I told him about Greyfern and Miss Wilburn and how I had won a special prize for progress. He seemed pleased.

'And how did you get on with Grandad?'

I looked at him, and then I looked away. 'I don't think he liked me very much,' I said vaguely.

My father chuckled. 'And what makes you say that, old boy?'

But I just didn't want even to *think* about it any more. I shrugged. 'I'm ever so glad to be back,' I said.

'Well, we're glad to have you back.'

And that was that.

My first unexpected pleasure on my return was the discovery that I was now to have a bedroom all of my own. It had been newly distempered primrose yellow and its window looked out over the croquet lawn. It also shared a wall with my father's and Betty's room which wasn't so good. Without trying to listen I could not help but overhear their voices—or, rather, Betty's—and during the years I occupied my little room I was destined to hear that deathly, soul-chilling voice rising and falling interminably, as I had once heard the sea gnawing at the Chesil Bank.

My father had hung two pictures on my wall, one at the foot of the bed and the other above the mantelpiece. Both were by the English Visionary artist Edward Calvert; one, a woodcut, titled, I believe, *The Cyder Harvest*; the other *The Primitive City*. They were tiny little pictures and at first I didn't think much of them, but the more closely I examined them the more I found there. Like windows into a strange and secret world—a curiously *private* world—they gave me the oddest sense that I was a sort of Gulliver with my eye to some Lilliputian keyhole. And I could never quite make out what those minute little citizens of *The Primitive City* were actually *doing*. None of them seemed to be paying the least attention to the others. One—a girl—had just got out of a river and appeared to be drying herself on a towel. Beside her was a tree loaded down with apples or fruits of some kind, each one at least as big as her head. Another girl was driving an ox cart over a bridge. And in the background were the most extraordinary houses—or was it, in fact, a castle?—and little people going up stairs or vanishing into archways or drawing up buckets of water from a well. Everyone seemed so busy, so preoccupied, and so obviously *happy*. In the end I grew so fond of them all that I wouldn't have changed those two pictures for anything.

I daresay I would have been able to if I'd wished for the Old Rectory was full of paintings. Many of them were by my Uncle Richard—portraits and landscapes and still-lifes in oils and watercolours—which were eventually to kindle in me the desire to be a painter myself. Richard was a fine artist with a genuine lyrical vision, and without my being aware of it his work set for me a standard of excellence by which I was later able to measure and weigh much that was merely meretricious. But above all I revered his response to the magic of landscape. Like Fuseli confronted by a Constable, Richard's sketches made me feel like reaching for my umbrella. He captured in paint what I could only feel.

I had been back at home less than a week before my father dropped another casual bombshell in my lap. And, just as before, it was my asking about my dog which gave him his cue. I raised the subject at lunch one day, having been prompted to do so by Ruby. Before he had had a chance to frame a reply Betty said: 'Oh, you're not having one.'

'But . . .' I stammered, turning to my father. 'But you *promised*! When I got back from Brighton, you said!'

At least my father had the decency to look uncomfortable. 'Well, you see, old boy, the snag is you'll be going away to school next month and, well, you wouldn't be able to look after him then, would you?'

I stared at him as if I'd just seen him plain for the first time. 'You *knew*!' I cried. 'You knew all the time! And you *still* promised!'

'Oh no,' he protested, 'that's not true. We only decided to send you to the Grammar School while you were away in Brighton.'

All my bitterness boiled over. 'It's not *fair*!' I wailed. 'It's not *fair*! You wouldn't have done it to Weg! You . . . you . . .' Emotion choked me. I pushed back my chair and stumbled, howling, out of the room.

That time I really did get through to him. I heard him calling after me but I simply didn't want to know. I kept on running until I got to the fens and there I hid myself.

Afterwards I learnt from Rue that it was Betty who had put her foot down about the dog, and remembering her reaction when I had first broached the subject I wasn't surprised. Oddly enough, deep down, I don't think I had ever truly *believed* that I would be allowed one. It was altogether too rich a dream ever to become real. I should have left it that way.

But the incident did have a very marked effect on my relation with my father. It wasn't exactly that I felt I could no longer trust him—*au fond* I both could and did—but that I no longer dared to put that trust to the test. In the last resort I knew he would not abandon me, but how could I be certain that I had reached that last resort? My experiences in Brighton had not all been happy but, thanks to Aunt Doll, I had survived them. Very well then, from now on I would simply have to grit my teeth and hang on grimly, come what may.

I gathered that I was to be sent to Thretford Grammar School for Boys as a weekly boarder. In strict confidence I asked Rue if she knew why this was. After all, Thretford was only eight miles from Larling and several local children bicycled to the station and caught the school train every morning. Why not me too? She did not know and I was still too tender to risk asking my father lest he change his mind again and decide to send me away altogether.

I was taken in to Norwich and kitted out with a school uniform; grey flannel suit and shirt, black and yellow stockings, even—God save the mark!—a cap and a tie. I gazed dolefully at myself in the long mirror. The pimply shop assistant patted my bottom, said I was 'a fine little man', and kept slipping his hand between my legs to ascertain whether I was 'comfortable'. He had terribly bad breath and I was glad when the fitting was over. My father thoughtfully presented me with a second-hand copy of *Tom Brown's Schooldays* which he had bought from a bookstall in the market for two pence. I started reading it as soon as we got back home and by the evening I felt even more despondent.

On September 20th Bodge loaded my trunk into the back of our Austin saloon and my father drove me over to Thretford. He had just started work on his autobiography—*Between Two Worlds*—and he occupied the journey by reminiscing about his own schooldays at Christ's Hospital. He seemed to have enjoyed them. Remembering Grandpa I wasn't altogether surprised.

We pulled up outside the Headmaster's house and, a minute later, I was being introduced to Mr G—. I thought I had never in my life seen anyone who looked so like a pig in clothes. He was a very large man with sandy hair, tiny little pale blue eyes and an upturned nose which was really nothing more nor less than a snout. Little tufts of curly reddish hair sprouted out of each nostril, from deep within each ear, and even bushed out at the tops of his mottled cheeks. He pumped my father by the hand and bared his yellow teeth at me in what was no doubt intended to be a jovial grin. 'We'll get someone to show you your digs, young man. Come along in, Mr Middleton Murry. Whisky or sherry?'

My father winked at me and disappeared into a room

behind Mr G—. The door closed with a thud and a click. I looked up at the picture on the wall beside me. It was a photograph of a sports team. In the middle of the front row was seated the gross and unmistakable figure of Mr G—. His massive thighs were nutcrackering a rugby ball. His striped shirt was unbuttoned and curly hair was thrusting up eagerly through the vent like mustard and cress.

'And who are you?'

I spun round. A pretty, brown-haired woman in a grey dress smiling down at me from half-way up the stairs. 'I'm Col, Miss,' I said. 'Col Murry.'

'Karl?'

'No, "Col". It's not my real name though.'

'Well, what *is* your real name?'

'John. John Middleton Murry.'

'Oh, yes.' She nodded. 'I remember. Have you come all by yourself?'

'My father brought me. He's in there.' I pointed to the door.

'With the Headmaster?'

'Yes, Miss,' I said. 'He said someone would show me my digs.'

She smiled and descended to the foot of the stairs. 'You'd better come with me, John. I'll introduce you to Matron.'

She opened another door and then pushed a second one which was immediately behind it and was covered in green baize. I followed her, clutching my new, navy blue raincoat. The baize door wuffed to behind me. We passed down a dimly lit corridor and into an untidy room where a snub-nosed boy with brown, curly hair and light brown eyes was sitting at a table writing a letter. 'Oh, Raymond,' said my guide. 'This is John Murry, a new boy. Would you take him up to Matron, please?'

'Yes, ma'am.' He stood up, screwed on the top of his fountain pen and slipped it into an inside pocket.

Mrs G— smiled at me. 'You can leave your coat here if you like.'

Raymond held the door open for her politely and, when she had vanished through it, turned to me and looked me up and down. 'Are you Scots?'

'No,' I said. 'I don't think so.'

'You must be. Murray's a Scots name. You aren't very big are you?'

'No,' I agreed. 'Not very.'

'I shall call you "Midget". Midget Murray.' He laughed. 'My name's Machan—"Mac" to you. Are you a termer or a weeker?'

'?'

'A *boarder*. Weekly or termly boarder?'

'Oh. Weekly.'

'Lucky devil. What form are you in?'

'I don't know.'

'Well, how old are you?'

'Eight and a half.'

'Bloody hell!' he laughed. 'No wonder you're small.' He led me up a flight of uncarpeted wooden stairs and along a landing. 'That's the dorm in there,' he said. 'Want to look?'

I peered into a long low room which had about twenty iron beds lining the two longest walls. One bed was separated from the rest and placed in the middle of the short wall nearest to the door. 'That's George's,' said my guide. 'He's House Prefect. That's mine over there.'

I nodded. 'Where are all the others?'

'Most of 'em'll be coming on the four o'clock train. I came a day early—worse luck. My home's in Singapore. I only go back for the summer. Where's yours?'

'Larling.'

'Where's that?'

I told him.

He looked astonished. 'What are you boarding for then?'

'I don't know,' I confessed.

'You don't know anything, do you, Midget?'

I blushed shyly.

Mac introduced me to Matron. 'His name's Midget Murray,' he said. 'He's Scots too—from Lanarkshire. His father owns a grouse moor and a private aeroplane.'

'Och away wi ye, Master Machan,' she retorted. 'He's nae mir Scots than you are. Where's your luggage, laddie?'

'In the car, I think, Matron.'

'It's no use asking him,' said Machan. 'He doesn't know anything.'

'Off wi' ye, sauce box. Go and find Tom and tell him to bring the lad's box up here.'

Mac grinned at me and sauntered off, whistling jauntily.

'That scamp's the cheek o' the de'il,' sighed Matron philosophically.

I saw my father briefly before he left. He bent down to kiss me goodbye and then, presumably, thought better of it and gripped me by the shoulder instead. 'Anything you need, old boy, just let me know.'

I nodded and, with a final grin, he got into the car and drove off. I watched him out of sight then turned and made my way back up the steps to the Headmaster's house. Mr G— who had come out to see my father off caught hold of me deftly by the ear and spun me round. He jerked his thumb towards a distant gate. '*That* way, young man,' he said.

I got the message.

14

I SOON realized that the residential accommodation provided for boarders at Thretford Grammar School for Boys was of the type known euphemistically as 'basic'. Besides the single dormitory there was a dining room and the common room in which I had been introduced to Ray Machan. At the side of the house was a long, dark, wooden hut which was divided into two rooms. The smaller of these was called the locker room and here the boarders kept their sports gear and their coats together with such odd personal possessions as tuck boxes. Adjoining it was the prep room which was set out with rows of ancient and eroded desks. In front of the desks was a scarred and battered table at which the duty master sat. There were also two loathsome lavatories about which the legend prevailed that no one ever used them for shitting in because they smelt so abominable that you spewed up as soon as you got inside; consequently you never had anything left to shit out. They were known collectively as 'the bog'.

One of the first things I discovered was that bullying was endemic. This did not surprise me—after all, had I not just read *Tom Brown's Schooldays*?—but, being both young and small, I came right at the very end of the pecking order. The boy immediately senior to me suffered dreadfully. He was a sad, rabbity-looking creature, with blond curly hair, a damp pointy nose and pink-rimmed, watery eyes. He had a pronounced lisp and his knees always looked chapped. In the winter his fingers were lumpy with chilblains. His name was Reggie E— and he was the chosen prey of an exceptionally unpleasant senior boy called 'Stubbo'.

Stubbo had a sly, puffy face, the colour of uncooked dough, lank white hair, bitten-down nails, and a nose that looked like the lid of a pepper-pot so numerous were its blackheads. His fellow seniors cold-shouldered him, perhaps because they were afraid of catching something nasty. Stubbo took his rejection out upon Reggie. Most evenings after prep he would signal to Reggie who would give a sort of sickly smile and turn even paler. Then they would vanish into the bog. A quarter of an hour later they would emerge—Stubbo looking slyer than ever; Reggie looking pink-eyed and tearful.

One evening I asked Ray Machan what they did in there. He gave me a pitying look. 'Stubbo makes Reggie suck him off.'

'Oh,' I said.

Mac's lip twitched. 'Hasn't he tried to get you yet?'

'No.'

'You're lucky. Stubbo's got a prick like a marrow.'

'You mean Reggie actually *sucks* it?' The notion mystified me.

'That's right.'

'But *why*, Mac?'

'Why don't you ask him?'

But I didn't ask Reggie. I knew perfectly well why he did it. He was simply terrified of Stubbo and I, in my turn, was being terrorized by Reggie.

The methods were different. Stubbo used the threat of his superior physical strength; Reggie employed psychology. Behind that bulging forehead of his was a remarkable acute brain. He was in the class above me and had formed around himself a sort of secret society which he had equipped with codes and passwords and secret signs. He called himself 'Doctor Fu', based on the character 'Fu Manchu' in the novels of Sax Rohmer. During break Reggie and his cronies would foregather in a corner of the playground and he would issue his directions for the day's activities. One of his favourite pastimes was to order them to 'Get Midge'.

It was no use my trying to run away and hide. Sooner or later they would corner me and close in. Sweating with fear I would be frog-marched off into the shrubbery where Reggie was waiting. 'Tho,' he would whisper. 'Who have we here? A thpy?'

'I'm not a spy,' I would protest tearfully. 'Really I'm not.'

'Thay "thir" when you addreth me.'

'I'm not a spy—sir.'

'Thoon,' murmured Reggie thoughtfully, 'he will confeth. Tie hith handth.'

My arms were screwed round behind my back, my wrists lashed together with my school tie, and I was forced down on to my knees.

Sometimes Reggie would go to work on me with a pin, sometimes with a piece of string, sometimes with his bare hands. He had a genuine talent for devising tortures and one of my fingernails is still mis-shapen from a pin wound which went septic. But I could stand almost any amount of physical pain, and Reggie, realizing this, soon changed his tactics. I was sent to Coventry. My own classmates were forbidden to talk to me on pain of dire retribution from 'the Doctor'. I became a pariah, an untouchable, and I began to believe that the endless night was truly closing in upon me.

I tried every way I could think of to buy my way into Reggie's favour. I became an adept at pilfering from the local sweetshop and keeping him supplied with Mars bars and sherbert fountains. Alas, his appetite grew with what it fed upon and his demands rose ever higher. Once, in sheer desperation, I swiped a whole box of sherbert fountains—there must have been at least three dozen of them—and presented him with the loot. Even he was alarmed and, presumably out of fear that the theft would be discovered and traced to himself, he forced me to smuggle them back. And I did! Heaven knows what the sweetshop owner thought of it. Perhaps she believed in fairies.

Oddly enough this piece of bravado procured me what I longed for—a place in Reggie's gang. It was never a very secure place and when Reggie was in need of diversion he would often whistle up his tame dogs and set them on me, but at least I was acknowledged, and life became intermittently tolerable. However, by then, no doubt largely as a result of my social misfortunes, my schoolwork had fallen off dreadfully. In my second term I found myself 'on Satisfecit'. This meant that I had to carry round with me a blank copy of the weekly timetable and, at the end of each lesson, persuade the master in charge to initial the appropriate square as an indication that my work had been satisfactory. On Monday mornings, directly after prayers, those 'on Satisfecit' queued up to present their papers to the Headmaster. For each blank space on his timetable the malefactor received a cut with a cane.

We boarders were fortunate in that one of our middle-school boys was a skilled forger. His name was Leslie Abbot. For a nominal fee, such as cleaning his shoes for him, Abbot

John Middleton Murry,
Violet, Col and Weg

On the golf course at Yateley

Above:
The Old Rectory, Larling

Left: Bodge

would fill in the gaps on your Satisfecit with perfect facsimiles of any master's initials. It was a risk, of course, but having once felt the weight of Mr G—'s mighty arm behind a malacca cane, you took the risk gladly.

Then one day an awful thing happened. I lost my Satisfecit form. I had left it in my locker at Saturday lunchtime before catching the train home and when I went to collect it on the Monday morning it had disappeared. There was no time to beg Abbot to produce a complete faked sheet even if he had been able to do it. All I could do was to confess to Mr G— that I had lost it and I well knew what that meant. Sick with apprehension I took my place at the end of the dismal queue. When I reached the Headmaster he held out his plump hand for my Satisfecit. As I tried to explain what had happened his lips curled into a sneer of disbelief. 'I think you're lying, Murry.'

'No, sir. I'm not, sir. Really, sir.'

'Would you be arguing with me?'

What could I say? I simply hung my head.

Mr G— really enjoyed his Monday morning exercise. It set him up for the week ahead. He removed his mortarboard and gown, took off his jacket and rolled up his sleeves. Then he commanded his victim to bend down and catch hold of the bottom rail of the gym wall-bars. The cane didn't swish through the air—it roared. *Whack!* A gasp of sucked-in breath. *Whack!* And so it went on.

I was last in the line. Only Mr G— and I, and a solitary duty prefect were left in the gym. By now Mr G— was nicely warmed up, his face a-glow from his exertions, a silvery snail-streak of spit shining on his chin. He signed to me to take my place and, as I did so, he prodded my behind with the ferrule of his cane and addressed a little homily to me. 'We have the best of reasons for believing that you are the ringleader of a gang in the lower-school, Murry. I am now about to demonstrate to you just how much this school disapproves of gangs.'

His third swipe caught me across the back of the thighs and hurt so much that I let go of the bar and sank to the floor.

Perhaps because of this the fourth landed in the middle of my back. For the last two the attendant prefect was obliged to hold me in place.

Mr G—'s breathing was heavy; possibly post-coital. 'Now go . . . back to . . . your class . . . boy!' he panted.

I began to straighten up and was promptly sick.

The prefect, whose name was Dyce, was a blue-chinned six footer. He picked me up, carted me across the playground to the washrooms and shoved my head under the cold water tap. 'Jesus Christ, kiddo,' he muttered not unkindly. 'That was some tanning.'

I missed the first lesson that morning and I was still pretty groggy at break. Mr Wheeler, the French master, asked me if I was feeling ill and sent me off to see Matron. I didn't go. Instead I crept into the locker room and lay down on a pile of coats. After a bit I got up and went across to my locker. The first thing I saw when I opened the door was my Satisfecit! I really believe that if Reggie had been there when I discovered it I would have tried to kill him, though, naturally, when I accused him of having taken it he swore he didn't know what I was talking about.

There was an epilogue to this incident. Six days after my beating the bruises were still there. When I got home on the following Saturday Rue came into the bathroom while I was having my bath. She caught sight of my back and let out a wail of dismay. 'What *have* they done to you, Karl?'

'I was caned,' I said. 'But it's all right now. It doesn't hurt any more.'

But Rue's dander was up. She ran downstairs and fetched my father and Betty to see me. At first I refused to show them my bruises. My motives were mixed. I didn't want my father to know that I'd been punished, but far more was I terrified lest he should make a scene about it and get me into worse trouble.

They extracted the story from me by degrees, though I was careful not to breathe a word about Reggie. I begged my father not to do anything but he just looked grim and told me not to worry. 'You won't write a letter to Mr G—, will you?' I pleaded.

He assured me he wouldn't and, slightly easier in my mind, I went to bed.

What he did do was to get into the car, drive straight over to Thretford, and confront Mr G—. Fortunately for my peace of mind I did not discover this till long afterwards. By then both Mr G— and I had left Thretford for ever and the school had become a quite different place. Even so I think I guessed that something *had* happened because I was taken off Satisfecit and, when in the spring term of my second year, I became a termly boarder, Mr G— was almost affable. He even went so far as to address me as 'young Middleton' and to congratulate me on having won a medal in the school sports. For my part I remained somewhat diffident.

15

COMPARED to the desperation of my life at Thretford, conditions back home at Larling seemed almost tranquil. They were, of course, nothing of the sort, but the tension there was of a different kind and I always had the solace of the woods and the fens. Furthermore, just before Christmas '34, my father sailed to the U.S.A. on a lecture tour. He was away for three months and without his actual physical presence in the house to stimulate her, Betty's rages were slightly less demoniacal. Undoubtedly it was Weg who suffered most at this time. Never for a moment did Betty let her forget that she was subordinate to Mary in every way. From being the carefree companion of our early days together at Larling, Weg had become a timid and mouse-like little creature who slipped softly about the house, terrified of drawing attention to herself. She had good reason to be afraid for Betty was quite capable of attacking her savagely with whatever weapon happened to hand. Forlorn and bewildered, poor Weg tried her hardest to please, and during her school holidays she became a sort of unpaid drudge, scrubbing and polishing to Betty's directions. Quite suddenly she seemed much older than I was. Not fully comprehending why this was, I added to the burden of her unhappiness by preferring young Mary as a companion.

One day, made desperate by misery, Weg ran away to the de Jongs. Steppie brought her back and thereafter Weg must have thought herself in Hell indeed. She never forgave Steppie this act of betrayal, though it is difficult to see what else Steppie could have done in the circumstances. Nevertheless, my sympathies on this occasion were all with Weg. I knew what it must have cost her to take the plunge, but I also knew something she didn't, namely that escape was for ever impossible because, sooner or later, *everyone* was bound to betray you.

As usually happened when he was away from home for any length of time my father contrived to forget what life was like when he was there. In fact his journal entries made while he was returning on board *The Majestic* at the beginning of March almost make one weep at his powers of self-deception. Betty emerges from them as a sort of beautiful *vision en rose*, infinitely tender, warm, and loving. Undoubtedly a good deal of this fervour can be attributed to the fact that he had been celibate for nearly three months, but it is painful to reflect that almost at the very moment when he was penning his wistful dreams his "beloved" was laying into his ten year old daughter with an ebony ledger rule and shrieking at the top of her voice that she was nothing but 'a sly, lazy, ugly, ungrateful little bitch' who took after her 'filthy father'.

Nevertheless, the warmth of my father's pleasure at seeing her again satisfied even Betty. For a little while at least an uneasy sort of peace descended on the household. Betty herself even went so far as to suggest that I might invite a school friend to stay with me during the Easter holidays. My father nodded benignly. 'Yes, go ahead, old boy. Why don't you?'

'All right,' I said. 'Thanks. I will.'

My choice alighted upon Richard B—. He was the only son of a bank manager in Thretford and, like myself, occupied a somewhat precarious position on the fringes of Reggie's gang. He was, however, more fortunate than I in that he was a day boy. I had been to his house several times on free afternoons, and on one of these occasions his father had shown me a slab of concrete in the cellar which, he said, had been cracked in half by an earthquake. I was suitably impressed.

The invitation was duly issued and, rather to my surprise, Richard accepted. He made it a condition that I was to come back to Thretford to stay with him immediately afterwards. Everything went well. Betty was on her best behaviour; Richard and I climbed trees, erected a tent in the meadow, made camp fires and fried eggs which we stole from Mr Lumley's barn. It was all surprisingly 'normal' and, in due course, I was packed off in my turn to stay with the B—s.

Mrs B— had made up another bed for me in Richard's room, contending that this would be cosier and more convenient. Certainly Richard and I were not averse to the arrangement. On the first evening we each set about compiling a list of all the dirty words we could think of. Then we compared our lists and combined them into a sort of *codex maximus* which, considering our ages, must have been quite an impressive document. I had a marked advantage in that I had Betty's familiar vocabulary to draw on even though I didn't know what some of the words meant or even how to spell them. My rendering of 'gamahuche' was, as I recall it, almost Elizabethan in its flamboyant idiosyncrasy. Naturally Richard challenged it, but since there was no arbiter to whom we could appeal it got in by default.

Later on we took our bath together. This was rendered more exciting by our making the water cloudy with soap then submerging ourselves up to our chins while Richard sang an erotic version of the lyric to *'Twas on the Isle of Capri* which he had composed. As his angelic treble described in lascivious detail what he had found beneath the old apple tree, so our little periscopic pricks would rise, jerking manfully above the surface of the soapy water; his, golden grown and pointed; mine, pink, rounder and circumcised. We tickled each other's with our toes and had a gay old time.

When we were in bed Mr B— came up to say goodnight. He sat on Richard's bed and played the mouth-organ to us—*Pack Up Your Troubles In Your Old Kit Bag* and *Take Me Back to Dear Old Blighty*. He had been an officer in the trenches on the Western Front and he still looked the part. I liked him a lot.

On the final night of my stay Mr B— appeared in our bedroom as usual. I settled back against my pillows all ready for him to tell us about how the 'Minnie' had exploded in the mouth of the dugout killing the Duty Corporal and burying them all for a day and a night. But this time Mr B— had other things on his mind. In clipped, military phrases he informed us that we were two of the foulest-minded little boys it had ever been his misfortune to encounter. He suggested we would be well-advised to scrub our tongues with carbolic soap and wash out our mouths with Jeyes' fluid. He told us he was shocked and disgusted by us, that we were a living abomination in the eyes of all clean-living, right-thinking men. To lend substance to his words he produced from his wallet our crumpled and forgotten *codex maximus*. Holding it by one corner he struck a match and set fire to it before our eyes. Like Thomas Cranmer he even encouraged the flames to lick his fingers as if to purge them of the contaminating filth. When the list was consumed to the last frail feather of ash he clicked his heels, did an about turn, and marched out of the room.

Richard and I eyed each other apprehensively and then both burst into hysterical giggles. We stuffed our pillows into our mouths and writhed and twisted in an agony of near-asphyxiation. Finally Richard found the breath to gasp out: 'It's a . . . bloody good thing . . . he wasn't . . . *listening at the bathroom keyhole*!'

When I saw Richard again at the beginning of the summer

term I asked him what had happened after I'd left. 'Oh, it wasn't too bad,' he said. 'I told him you'd written the list. It seemed the best way out.'

'Did he believe you?'

Richard grinned. 'Oh yes. He said he'd always suspected you came from thoroughly bad stock.'

16

WAS I a particularly 'foul-minded' little boy? The question poses problems of definition which preclude any straightforward answer. My knowledge of the euphemistically termed 'facts of life' was certainly extensive and I was able to put several of my contemporaries straight on the mysterious ritual of their own conception. However, since none of us was yet capable of producing sperm, they remained somewhat sceptical. Not that our failure was due to any lack of effort. We massaged our own and each other's penises with the same, single-minded endeavour that we devoted to the construction of paper gliders or planning a raid on the local sweetshop but, lacking the visible evidence, our claims for having achieved orgasm had to be taken on trust. One of our number whose father was a local G.P. brought along a medical directory to our hideout among the long grass on the edge of the school playing field. There we pored over the diagrams of the female reproductive system and woefully mispronounced such succulent items as *ostium urethrae* and *praeputium clitoridis* while our seniors watched the cricket and clapped sporadically. It was all very English.

One dozy afternoon during the annual Staff v. Students match, a patrolling prefect stumbled across us when we were sitting cross-legged in a tight little circle measuring each other's erections and comparing circumferences with a carefully calibrated length of white cotton. He clipped a couple of us lethargically round the ear and told us we were letting the school down by our failure to encourage the First XI. Then he caught sight of the notebook in which Reggie had been thoughtfully recording the vital statistics for posterity. He ran his eye down the column of figures; grinned; told us we were a lot of bloody little liars; chucked the book back at us; and strode off, god-like, on his rounds.

Generally speaking, sexual experiment at Thretford was confined to those in one's own age group. Occasionally you consulted your seniors, as I had consulted Mac about Stubbo and Reggie, but for the rest you made and shared discoveries with your coevals. Nor was there much attempt on the part of the seniors to corrupt us. I soon gathered that Stubbo's practises were disapproved of by the senior boarders but, on the other hand, Reggie was such an unprepossessing specimen that the general attitude seemed to be that a worm deserved no better fate.

After lights-out in the dormitory there was a fair amount of discussion of sexual topics and at least an equal amount of masturbation, but we juniors were left pretty much to our own devices. Mostly these were not of a sexual nature at all. Ray Machan was fond of reading thrillers and, night after night, he would retail these to us in serial form. Thus I sweated fearfully through Sapper's *Four Rounds with Bulldog Drummond*, *The Hound of the Baskervilles* and several of Richard Hannay's adventures. So accurate was Mac's memory that when I eventually came to read some of these tales for myself I found that I already possessed a very fair knowledge of their characters and their involved plots.

Ray Machan's was by no means the only talent among the boarders at Thretford. The one I found most fascinating was undoubtedly Leslie Abbot's. Besides being a skilled forger, Abbot, who was a fourth former and at least five years senior to me, was one of those curiously detached individuals who seem able to construct and inhabit a private and particular world of their own. He was fair-haired and had large, thin, round ears which stuck out almost at right angles from his long, humorous face. His white-lashed eyes were grey and when you asked him something he had a way of looking at you as though he were considering, one by one, at least a dozen separate answers to your simple question.

Abbot was always engaged upon some interesting and mysterious project; either devising patent invisible inks, or tinkering with pungent chemicals in his desk in the far corner of the prep room, or constructing elaborate burglar alarm systems with batteries and bulbs and buzzers and yards and yards of thin, cotton-bound, copper bell-wire. He had fixed up an intricate system of thread, cotton reels and elastic bands by which he contrived to send messages during prep to his friend Roger Campbell who occupied a desk in the opposite corner at the back of the room. The two of them spent at least half of one term designing and constructing a series of Heath-Robinsonish traps to combat a plague of mice in the locker room.

My own favourite among Abbot's numerous contrivances was a simple device worked by a concealed string and a piece of elastic whereby he could tip his straw hat in salute to members of the staff without actually having to take his hand out of his trousers pocket in order to do it. This seemed to me to strike the sort of perfect balance between insolence and humility that only a mind as subtle and devious as his could possibly have dreamt up. In Abbot I recognized, with aching envy, one who was prepared to take on society single handed and force it to accept his own terms.

The spell of (relative) tranquillity that had settled over the Old Rectory since my father's return from the States lasted until the summer holiday. Betty had already decided that we were to spend this at Barmouth in Wales. Some ancestors of hers had once been tenant farmers at a place called Cors-y-gedol where, as a child, she had enjoyed some happy times.

My father booked rooms in a boarding house and arranged with the Deiners that they should join us there. We arrived at tea time after a hot and exhausting 260 mile drive from Norfolk during which Weg had earned Betty's displeasure by being car-sick. Scarcely were we disembarked before Betty was finding fault with the accommodation. Probably she was justified but it seemed all too like the first hint of the overcast that presages a coming storm. And so it proved. From that moment on she did her utmost to make the holiday as miserable as possible for everyone concerned. For no reason at all poor Rue was singled out for a series of spiteful attacks which culminated in Betty screaming abuse at her down the stairs. It took all our concerted efforts to prevent Rue from catching the next train home. Our only respite came when the adults went off for the day rambling over the mountains. Left to ourselves we soon discovered a fun-fair, and thereafter spent much of our time and all our pocket money gambling on the penny slot machines.

It was during this grim 'holiday' that my father finally decided that he would attempt to found a permanent 'Socialist Centre'—"a place where men and women loved one another without possessiveness". The idea—or something very like it—had been in and out of his mind for years, and the dawning realization that, whatever he did, he would never be able to live any sort of reasonable life with Betty, at last drove him to try to make the concept into reality. My own suspicion is that The Adelphi Centre owed its birth at least in part to D. H. Lawrence's Pantisocratic 'Rananim'—that wistful dream of an ideal community where a chosen group of friends would live out their lives in perfect fulfilment. And perhaps a little to its counterpart the 'Heron Farm'—the never-never land with which my father and the dying Katherine Mansfield had once solaced her unhappy spirit.

On his return from Barmouth my father immediately set about canvassing support for The Adelphi Centre from among his friends. As always when his heart and mind were working in concert, his passionate conviction in the importance of the enterprise carried him forward irresistibly. It was, as he remarked in his journal, "the excitement of the early days of the old *Adelphi* all over again", and for a brief period even Betty was caught up in his enthusiasm. Soon the donations began rolling in. By November *The Adelphi School Company* had been set up; The Oaks—a large Victorian mansion in the village of Langham five miles north of Colchester—had been purchased; and a new chapter in our lives seemed about to begin.

In fact the only immediate difference the founding of The Adelphi Centre made to my own life was that it brought a host of new visitors down to Larling. Some of them like the cheerful, bearded architect Butling, were to be the founding fathers of the new enterprise. Others were less easy to categorise. Among these latter was a young writer. Let us call him 'Osbert Marigold'. He appeared shortly after we returned from Wales and we did not know what to make of him at all. I imagine he must have been in his early twenties; pale and unprepossessing of feature, with lank, floppy hair which he wore longer and more dandruffy than most, and an unnerving habit of whinneying shrilly at his own erudite jokes. He stayed with us for about a month and, in between periods of resting upstairs on his bed, he dabbled in various forms of self-expression. These included the performance of ballet-type exercises on the croquet lawn and some painful attempts at wood carving which terminated abruptly when he succeeded in wounding himself with a gouge.

I watched my father closely to see how he was reacting to this improbable soul-brother and soon detected unmistakable signs of mild exasperation. My reading was confirmed one afternoon when we were gathering damsons in the orchard. My father, having climbed up into the laden tree, shook the branches; then Weg, Mary and I moved in, scooped up the fruit and shovelled it into baskets. By and by Osbert wandered up and after watching us working for a while delivered himself of some (presumably witty) observation in Latin. A moment later a veritable cloudburst of ripe damsons had descended upon his head. 'Sorry about that,' apologized my father. 'I slipped.' I glanced up into the tree and was treated to one of his rare and enormous winks of complicity.

Osbert soon made it clear to us that the only subject he

found of surpassing interest was Osbert. Certainly he had very little time for children. He also succeeded, in a quite remarkably short time, in getting on the wrong side of Bodge and Ruby. This was foolish of him for, shortly afterwards, he was afflicted with constipation and applied to Rue for an aperient. Still smarting from her slight she mixed him up a dose of Epsom salts that would have unblocked the Suez Canal. Next morning, finger pressed to her lips, she beckoned Weg and me to the ventilator window of the downstairs toilet. Agog we listened to the sounds of muffled detonations from within and to Osbert groaning aloud that he was dying. Betty was highly amused when she learnt of the episode. 'He's just a wet fart anyway,' was her somewhat unkind comment.

Occupied though he was both with The Adelphi Centre and the preparation of his lectures for his second tour of the United States, my father still found time to take an interest in our scholastic progress. A few probing questions having convinced him that I knew almost no arithmetic whatsoever he set himself the task of teaching me some. Roped together we assaulted the towering peak of long division. Eventually I made it to the summit and that achievement must rank among the greatest pedagogic triumphs of the age. He also decreed that Weg and I should each write him a weekly story. When Daphne Deiner, who had returned with us from Barmouth, begged to be included in on this, I could hardly believe my ears.

As the deadline for handing in our work approached I still had not produced a single line. Daphne, on the other hand, was already half way down her tenth sheet of foolscap. I was astounded and enquired timidly whether I might be allowed to read what she had written. She seemed almost flattered that I had asked, so I took the first nine sheets of *The Mystery of the Pyramids* and dived in. By the time I was into the second paragraph I was hooked. Daphne hadn't missed a trick. Secret passages, murders, trapdoors, hollow sphinxes, mysterious priest cults—you name it; she had it. I recognized the real thing when I saw it and hung over her shoulder while her pencil flew across the final page describing how the last poisoned dart pinged home in the Professor's neck. 'Daph,' I said humbly. 'That's marvellous.'

Daphne sniffed modestly, but looked pleased. 'It's not bad, is it?' she said and added, casually: 'My next one's going to be about diamond prospecting up the Amazon. I'm going to start it this afternoon.'

I wandered upstairs to the nursery, got out the pen and ink and a sheet of lined paper, only to find that Daphne's facility, instead of inspiring me to emulation, had reduced me to all but total impotence. At the end of an hour I had produced ten badly blotted lines about an unlikely trio called—believe it or not—Tom, Dick and Harry. I even gave them a dog called Rover for good measure. As I recall it I sent them sliding on a frozen pond, whereupon one—or was it all?—fell through the ice. Rover, an altogether admirable, not to say Herculean, hound, rescued them by dragging a dead branch to the edge of the hole and then hauling them out. I read it through and winced inwardly. The odd thing was that in my mind's eye I could so clearly 'see' what I described as happening: the sunlight was shimmering from the encrusted, blue-shadowed snow; Rover's pink tongue was quivering like a slice of animated ham; in my head it was all real and alive-oh; but by the time I had transferred it on to paper it was even deader than Daphne's professor. I appended an apologetic postscript: 'Sorry, I can't seem to write stories,' sneaked my shameful offering downstairs and slipped it in under Daphne's ten pages and Weg's four.

My father was kindness itself. When I got my abortion back I found he had written across the bottom in his incredibly neat and miniscule script, 'Rover seems a very *strong* dog.' Many years later I asked him if he remembered this incident. He frowned thoughtfully and then his face broke into a wide smile. 'Good Lord, yes,' he chuckled. 'All those endless facile screeds of Daphne Deiner's! How I groaned in my soul when I saw yet another.'

Facile screeds? Groaned in his soul? That wasn't in the least how I remembered them.

17

THAT winter—December 1935—my father departed for his second lecture tour in America. This time he was to be away for four months. Before he left he told me that he had made arrangements for me to go to a new school in Gloucestershire in the following September, and that, until then, I was to be a termly boarder at Thretford. I pleaded to be left as I was but apparently his mind was made up. I could see no convincing reason for the change and I can see none now unless it was that he feared my presence was having a deleterious effect upon young Mary. Certainly she and I had grown very close to one another and, more than once, he had commented adversely upon this in his journal. Perhaps if I had been able to tell him exactly what life at Thretford was like he might have relented, but that was impossible.

Actually, being a full time boarder was not as bad as it might have been. For one thing, during the second week of term Reggie ran away from school. He had got half way to Norwich before he was found and brought back. The notoriety which this exploit focused upon him served to divert his attention from his perennial persecution of me. Furthermore, Stubbo, alarmed lest Reggie should divulge the reason for his flight, went out of his way to be pleasant to him. There were no more evening summonses to the bog, no more arm-twistings, no more 'Chinese burns'. Gradually Reggie began to emerge from his shell. Aided by an amused and condescending Abbot he set about constructing first an electric motor and then a crystal set. I was graciously permitted to assist him in these enterprises and soon was constructing a crystal set of my own. I thus discovered in myself a modest talent for practical mechanics and, at precisely the right moment, Ray Machan saw fit to lend me a volume of H. G. Wells' short stories. At one step my imaginative horizons expanded by light years. I got *The Mysterious Universe* by James Jeans out of the school library and grappled dizzily with the secrets of the cosmos. When I wrote a letter to my father, who was then in New York, I spent half of it retailing the plot of *The Time Machine* and urging him to read it. The other half of the letter I devoted to an account of my experiences in Grimes Graves.

Grimes Graves is the name given to an extraordinary labyrinth of neolithic flint mines burrowed into the deep chalk at the village of Brandon just outside Thretford. One afternoon at the beginning of March the History master escorted the two most junior forms on a visit to this archaeological curiosity. We watched two ancient, leather-aproned flint knappers at work chipping out flints for flintlock rifles. Apparently the war in Abyssinia had led to these craftsmen being called out of their retirement to manufacture spare parts for the weapons of the Abyssinian Nationalist forces. I must confess that it seemed a lost cause even to me.

After this we descended by means of a series of swaying ladders into a deep hole from the bottom of which a number of dark burrows disappeared into the chalk walls. Our guide explained that we would crawl after him into one of these burrows which the neolithic miners had scooped out thousands of years ago. We would follow him through the workings till we reached one of a dozen inner chambers where some ancient, reindeer-antler hand-picks which had recently been discovered were now on display. Our route was lit by candles set into niches in the tunnel walls at roughly twenty yard intervals.

I glanced up at the tiny scrap of daylight far above me and wished heartily that I had had the courage to stay up there at the risk of being called a coward. But it was too late for that now. The last of the party was already disappearing into one of the tunnels. I dropped on to my hands and knees and scuttled after him.

For some minutes all went well. It was rather like being inside a rabbit warren. I kept my eyes on the dim shape of the boy I was following and strained to catch the voice of the guide who was somewhere up ahead. Every now and again we passed other tunnels which branched off to left and right. Some of these were also lit by candles which flapped nervously as I crawled past. The History master had told us that the workings extended for miles.

Then—quite how it happened I'm still not sure—I lost sight of the boy in front of me. I believe one of my shoe-laces came untied and I stopped to do it up. As I crawled off again in pursuit of the party I found myself confronted by a 'Y' fork. I could still hear the guide's voice but, by some cruel acoustic trick, I could not be sure which branch of the tunnel it was coming from. 'Hey!' I yelled. 'Wait for me!' and set off at top speed down the right hand fork.

I could not have covered more than twenty yards before I realized that there were no more candles ahead. I understood at once what had happened and began to turn round. Small though I was the manœuvre was barely possible, and in executing it I dislodged the candle from its niche and it went out. The damp walls crowded in chokingly and I simply panicked, I screamed at the top of my voice. The terror I experienced at that moment was absolutely primeval—paralysing. It makes me sweat just to recall it.

Somehow I managed to get back to the junction, but by then I was quite incapable of thinking rationally. I set off down the left hand fork. Of course, what I should have done was to take the *right hand* fork. What I was now doing was heading back along the route by which we had entered.

How long I crawled around there on my own is difficult to say. It seemed like years. Probably it was not for more than a few minutes. When I was discovered I was in no state to give a coherent account of what had happened. The others thought it was a great joke but, try as I might, I just couldn't see the funny side of it. But it certainly cured me of any incipient inclinations towards spelaeology.

During that long and chilly Easter term news of Larling reached me via Rue's letters. She told me that she had started saving up for a new bike and that 'the Missis' was talking of going off on a Mediterranean cruise in the spring. 1936 promised to be an *annus mirabilis* indeed. In the event it proved to be all of that and then some more.

At this time, all unknown to me, my father was in the process of making a fundamental reappraisal of his life. Apart from young Mary, whom he worshipped nigh unto idolatry, his marriage to Betty had brought him nothing but disasters. Yet he, more than most men, *needed* to love a woman; needed the emotional security of a happy marriage; needed to trust in love. He had it in him to be a paragon among husbands and fathers. He often quoted with approval Blake's observation: '*Let the men do their duty, and the women will be such wonders!*' But Betty would not let him 'do his duty'. Her total possessiveness, her insane jealousy, her blind and terrifying rages simply would not allow him to prove what he might be. To me the astonishing thing is that he did not call it a day long before. His capacity for hope seemed all but inexhaustible. Time and time again he put on record in his journal that Betty really had turned over a new leaf and that he and she had reached a new understanding. It never lasted for much longer than a week. And out of his subconscious acceptance of the fact that the problem of his marriage was insoluble in ordinary human terms, The Adelphi Centre had been born.

It was the very success of this venture that encouraged him to reassess his own private situation and, being the man he was, he sought for a meaningful human relationship to complete the new social pattern he had discovered. He found what he thought he was seeking in Jimmy Young's wife, Helen, who had parted from Jimmy and was now living in New York. As he expressed it himself in a somewhat apocalyptic journal entry for April 19th, 1936: "So the wheel has come full circle. Out of my denial of my dream in my life with Betty came the energy to realize my dream in the Centre; out of that realization came the power to dissociate my dream *from* Betty. That was a death, indeed. The only possible relation with a woman now was one which grew out of the realization of the dream in the Centre, and the dissociation of it from any woman. Such a relation is now vouchsafed to me. . . ."

Was it only prudence which caused him to anagrammatize 'Helen' into 'Nehale' in his journal? Reading the entries for the final month of his stay in the States I am moved to wonder whether he was not in fact turning her into something or someone she could never be. But she offered him what he most needed when he was most sorely in need of it—tenderness. In one of the most moving, because it is among the most truly heartfelt passages in his journal at this time, he addresses us, his children, in these words: "—believe me when I tell you that, after 46 years of a life as bitter as most men have lived, only one thing matters; and that is *tenderness*. One could starve and it wouldn't *matter* if only one knew, beyond all doubt, that one was wrapped in the tenderness of someone's heart. Love, that calls itself love, and is not *tender* is just a *bloody blasphemy*." There he expresses exactly what it was that Betty could never give him. Totally insecure herself, she simply did not have it within her to give to anyone. By the time he sailed from New York on April 15th his mind was made up. He would make a new life for himself at the Centre where Helen would come to join him.

Though I was aware of none of this at the time, I soon gathered that something out of the ordinary was afoot. When I arrived home for the Easter holidays the talk seemed to be concerned mainly with Betty's preparations for her Mediterranean cruise, but there was also a considerable amount of to-ing and fro-ing between Larling and Langham. Weg and I accompanied my father on one of these trips and we were both very much impressed by the sheer size of The Oaks. We also met a number of familiar faces. Beside my Uncle Richard there was Butling the bearded architect, and the *fin de siècle* figure of Osbert Marigold.

On the drive back to Larling my father asked us casually how we would like to spend the summer holiday at the Centre.

'With you, Dadda?' enquired Weg carefully.

'Yes, of course.'

'I think I'd like it very much.'

'And how about you, old boy?'

'I thought we were going to go to the seaside,' I said.

'Well, we'd do that too, of course.'

'Honest?'

He nodded.

'O.K. then,' I agreed.

In his biography of my father F. A. Lea remarks of this period in my father's life—'It is neither desirable, nor necessary, nor even possible, to unwind the tangled skein of Murry's private life in the six weeks following his return from America.' If it was barely possible in 1958 when that book was written it is wholly impossible today since, in the meantime, my father's journals have been thoroughly censored and many of the references to Betty cut out and burnt. Judging from the fact that the pages covering the crucial weeks from the end of April to the beginning of May are all missing I can only suppose that during them my father must have informed Betty that she was to be supplanted by Helen Young. By then I was already back at Thretford and completely in the dark about what was happening at home. I recall receiving one postcard from Rue in which she referred guardedly to 'storms' and then, on my tenth birthday, another one which informed me that—'the Missis is going on her cruise tomorrow hooray'. Knowing how desperately Rue had been looking forward to this I rejoiced for her.

Even if Betty had been apprised of the true nature of the situation she must surely have discounted it. As far as my father was concerned her capacity for self-deception was prodigious. And, after all, as he himself has remarked, for five long years he had been "a veritable paragon of fidelity". Thus her shock on returning to Larling at the end of May and discovering that her husband really had left her for another woman must have been traumatic indeed. By all accounts she simply went berserk. Had Bodge not had the forethought to lock up the petrol cans in the generator house she would in all probability have razed Larling to the ground. As it was she smashed or burnt anything she knew my father still held precious, among them the beloved De Segonzac drawing which had been given to him by the artist during his early days in Paris. When this frenzied fit had worked itself out she bethought her of the one weapon which was ready to hand and which she knew could wound him as no other—Mary.

Even a superficial reading of my father's journals shows that it was on to his four year old daughter that he had diverted all the tenderness of feeling that her mother rejected. In a sense Mary had come to stand in for all of us in his affections. Certainly she had quite supplanted Weg. At the beginning of June my father, by then at Langham, is noting with real surprise "the new freedom and gaiety which has come to her (Weg) since the separation". This particular entry continues: ". . . it's rather a grim thought that I did not realize the full extent of the suppression imposed upon Weg at Larling. Nor do I think that I have recorded that on the day after I left Larling, when Weg came here for the first time for the week-end and I was feeling the separation from Mary very keenly indeed, she was barely sympathetic to me: and again I had not realized how Weg really felt about Mary. I do not mean to imply for one moment that Weg is not genuinely fond of Mary; but she had accumulated a fund of resentment at B's systematic preferring of Mary to herself, at being constantly compelled to subordinate herself to Mary." Had he written "B's *and my* systematic preferring of Mary" in that entry, instead of just "B's", he would have come even closer to the truth.

Betty's subsequent exploitation of Mary was as ruthless as it was devoid of subtlety. I had first-hand evidence of it during my half-term holiday which I spent in company with Weg at the Centre. The first evening I was there my father was summoned to the phone. He returned five minutes later looking pale and sick. It emerged that Betty had put Mary on the line to beg him to 'come home', and in the course of it she had wept bitterly. After that he made a point of never answering the phone himself until he had ascertained who was at the other end.

His sole means of contact with Larling was through Bodge, via our neighbours the Hewetsons, though Betty was forever ringing up the Centre and leaving dotty messages. One of the mildest of these was that she was making arrangements to put Mary into a convent and to become a Roman Catholic herself—presumably having discovered that the True Faith did not recognize divorce.

It then occurred to her that it might be useful to have me around at Larling as extra ammunition in the battle. She phoned me up at school and told me that from now on I was to come home at weekends. Having done this she could not resist informing my father how clever she had been; whereupon he swiftly frustrated the plan by decreeing that I should henceforward spend my weekends at Langham. So once more I became a weekly boarder and, incidentally, an adept at travelling without a railway ticket. Since my father was absent-minded to a fault about pocket-money—Weg and I hardly ever received any—my purloined fares provided a welcome boost to my finances.

Towards the end of June, by using May Deiner as a go-between, my father had somehow got Betty to agree to his seeing Mary in Norwich one Saturday afternoon. Weg, Virginia Young, and myself were to make up the party. Betty waited until all the arrangements had been completed and then sent a telegram stipulating that young Mary was not on any account to meet either Weg or myself. Not unnaturally my father chose to ignore this absurd fiat and we all spent a happy afternoon boating on the river Wensum. Mary was overjoyed to see us again but was obviously utterly bewildered by the emotional whirlpool into which she had been flung. I suspect, too, that underneath, I was almost as perplexed as she was. In a very real sense I had become a genuine competitor with my father for Mary's affections. She was the one person I knew (with the possible exception of Rue) who genuinely accepted me and appreciated me for what I was. I never had to put on any sort of an act with Mary and I knew I could trust in her affection absolutely. Yet I was also old enough to appreciate that, for my father, life with Betty was tantamount to a living death. What I did *not* understand was why, as a result of this, I had to be separated from Mary. I suppose I accepted it as just another of those bleak, inexplicable happenings which seemed to be woven right down the middle of my life.

When Betty learnt that Mary *had* met Weg and myself she was beside herself with rage and sent a furious message to The Oaks stating that my father would never be allowed to see Mary again. His reaction was to note in his journal: "I am coming to such a hatred and loathing of B. that I am terrified by it."

It was at about this time that he sent the following cable to Helen in New York:

PREPARE TO COME AND STAY FOR GOOD WITHIN ONE MONTH STOP HAVE CONSIDERED EVERYTHING STOP DECIDED WE MUST BE TOGETHER STOP THIS SEPARATION IS WASTE OF LIFE

18

IN the third week of July I left Thretford for good, convinced that however awful my next school might prove to be it could hardly be worse than what I had successfully survived. The things I had learnt there did not feature on the school curriculum; in fact the only lessons I remember were those when the English master read to us from Macaulay's *Lays of Ancient Rome*. I responded wholeheartedly to *Horatius* and *The Battle of Lake Regillus* and soon had great chunks of them off by heart. This time, however, sensible of my precarious situation, I kept the knowledge to myself. Only when I was well out of earshot would I risk declaiming:

Fast, fast, with heels wild spurning,
The dark grey charger fled;
He burst through ranks of fighting men;
He sprang o'er heaps of dead.
His bridle far outstreaming,
His flanks all blood and foam,
He sought the southern mountains,
The mountains of his home.
The pass was steep and rugged,
The wolves they howled and whined;
But he ran like a whirlwind up the pass,
And he left the wolves behind.

I also discovered to my surprise that the word 'quay' was pronounced 'key'.

I arrived at the Centre to find that everyone was frenziedly preparing for the first Adelphi Summer School which was due to open on August 1st. Weg had been spirited off to Belgium for a holiday by some friends of my father's and, with Mary at Larling, I was left very much on my own. Provided that I appeared at meal times nobody bothered very much about me. This suited me very well. I soon made friends with Butling's fiancée, a delightful, auburn-haired Canadian called Helen Deane who was in charge of the kitchens. She took me under her wing, sewed on my buttons and saw to it that I changed my underclothes from time to time but made no attempt to boss me about. So taken was I with Helen that I put it to her on one occasion that she might do worse than to marry my father. When she demurred I proffered the alternative suggestion that she might care to adopt me. 'I'm sure he wouldn't mind a bit,' I informed her cheerfully.

One afternoon Helen invited me to accompany her to Colchester on a shopping expedition. We ended up visiting the cinema. Besides the Laurel and Hardy feature film there was a newsreel of the fighting in Spain. I recall gritty shots of ordinary-looking men in shirt sleeves, rifles clutched in their hands, ducking and dodging among heaps of rubble. One stumbled and fell. He lay there in the roadway curled up as if asleep. I knew he was dead but even so it seemed a poor sort of battle compared with the cut and thrust of *Horatius*.

The outbreak of the Spanish Civil War, by lending a new and urgent perspective to the aims of The Adelphi Centre, undoubtedly contributed a great deal to the success of the first Summer School. Listening to the guests talking among themselves I learnt that they considered my father to be an important and significant figure and that another World War was apparently inevitable. My curiosity aroused I infiltrated myself into the back of the lecture hall and sat through an address on 'Militant Socialism' by my father of which I understood barely one word in ten. Thereafter I spent my time more profitably by taking on all comers on the putting course for 6d a go. I was well on the way to winning a modest reputation as a juvenile Henry Cotton when my father got wind of it. He marched out and sternly forbade any such capitalistic exploitation of the guests.

During August the Plowmans appeared at the Centre. Max had recently become the General Secretary of 'The Peace Pledge Union'—the pacifist fellowship inaugurated by the Reverend Dick Sheppard—and it was not long before he and my father were firm friends once more. Max was visibly impressed by the achievement of the Centre and no one could be warmer or more generous in praise than he. As for my father, his feelings are attested by his comment: "I regard it as the greatest triumph of the Centre that it has convinced Max of the necessity of its own existence." Curiously (and ominously!) one of the things which drew Max and my father together again was Max's appreciation of those very qualities in Betty which had first attracted my father to her. It was almost as though, at the very time when he most needed to be wholehearted, my father was glancing back over his shoulder and musing: 'Ah, if only . . .'

No sooner had the Summer School ended than the Plowmans insisted that my father and I must accompany them for a week's sailing on the Norfolk Broads, so, together with their son Piers, we drove to Wroxham and embarked aboard the gaff-rigged *Valkyrie IV*.

Today a sailing boat on the Broads is the exception rather than the rule and the waterways are reminiscent of a London rush-hour, but in 1936 there was hardly a motor cruiser to be seen. You sailed and, when the wind dropped, you 'quanted'. This entailed pushing a twelve foot pole into the mud at the river bottom, getting a firm grip on it, and then pacing sedately from prow to stern, pushing the boat along under you with your feet. Being too young to quant or sail I devoted myself to fishing. The first time I caught a fish I was so excited I promptly fell overboard. Thereafter the entry 'Cabin boy overboard' occurred with monotonous regularity in the pages of the ship's log which my father wrote up each evening.

Like most small boys I really did want to *admire* my father, not just feel sorry for him. In consequence I enjoyed that holiday more than any other I had ever spent with him. He loved sailing and had always dreamed of owning his own boat. Being skipper of a hired one, if only for a week, was for him a foretaste of paradise. For the first time I saw in him quite a different person from the rather remote and Olympian figure who had control over my destiny. He was gay and carefree and made jokes and listened quite seriously as I explained to him how you could tell the difference between the bite of a bream and a roach by the way the float moved.

One afternoon he rigged the dinghy and took me out with him on Horsea Mere for a sailing lesson. It was a far more successful lesson than any of our academic ones had been. He was delighted to find how quickly I got the knack of it and sang my praises to Max when we returned to *Valkyrie IV*. I doubt whether I have ever been happier.

To the best of my knowledge my father had never once spoken to me of Helen Young. Since, if things worked out as he intended, she would to all intents and purposes be my next step-mother within a month, this seems to me an odd oversight. Perhaps his experience the previous May when—all unknown to me at the time—he had engineered a meeting in Norwich between Weg and Helen, and Weg had been distinctly cool towards her, may have had something to do with it. Not that my reaction would necessarily have been the same as Weg's, but perhaps he just did not want to run the risk that it might be. What seems to me a far more likely reason is that, subconsciously, he was by no means convinced that Helen Young *was* the right woman for him. Had he been, there would surely have been no problem about putting me in the picture—after all it would merely have been another case of telling me what was about to happen, like my going to a new school. Yet he said nothing at all and, naturally, I did not ask.

While we were sailing and quanting around the Norfolk Broads the Deiners had rented a holiday bungalow at Walton-on-the-Naze some twenty miles from Langham. Thither they brought Ruby and Mary, and there, for a week or so, I joined them, thus enabling my father to keep his promise to me of 'a holiday by the sea'. It was from Rue that I learnt at first hand what life at Larling had been like since I was last there, with specific reference to the hair-raising scenes when Betty had returned from her cruise. What she told me made me very glad I had not been present.

My father came over to Walton and spent a night with us. When he had gone back to Langham Rue told me that she and Mary would be going to stay with some friends of my father's in Norwich. She added that she didn't think 'the Missis' was likely to let it happen. Knowing Betty as I did I could only agree with her.

In fact that plan was changed almost overnight. When we all returned to the Centre a few days later I learnt, again from Rue, that the Norwich scheme had been scrubbed. Now she and Mary were to go up to London to stay with some other friends of my father's, the Fierzes, who lived in Golders Green. Mary was to go to the King Alfred School in Hampstead and Rue was to be maid at the Fierz' house. Having long cherished an ambition to see London, Rue was obviously intrigued by the prospect. I don't recall Mary expressing any views on the matter.

The time for my departure to my new school was rapidly approaching and whenever I thought about it I felt sick in the stomach. I tried to find out something about the place from my father but apart from the fact that it was called Rendcomb College and was near Cirencester he was not able to tell me much. He did, however, assure me that it was a good school and that I would certainly be happy there. I was prepared to take his word on the first point; on the second I preferred to keep an open mind.

Just before I left the Centre two unfortunate incidents occurred. Both of them involved my father and, I daresay, one had a direct bearing upon the other. The first should not have involved him at all. It was a practical joke devised by Daphne Deiner and myself as a retaliation against Butling who had played one on us. It was a simple enough contrivance—a seaside pail full of water lodged on the top of a door. An urgent message was despatched to Butling that my father was anxious to see him and Daphne kept watch to signal his approach. At the signal I was to fix the bucket and retire. I got a signal all right—Daphne with one hand clasped over her mouth and the other waving wildly. The bucket was duly positioned and I stepped back. Slow footsteps approached, the door edged inwards and—God in Heaven!—it was my father! For a timeless second I saw him regarding me quizzically as I stood open-mouthed, frozen in shock. Then the water was sluicing over him, his spectacles were hanging from one ear, and the empty pail was lodged rakishly over one eyebrow. I heard a gale of unseemly laughter from behind him and became aware of the Machiavellian Butling absolutely beside himself with unholy mirth.

My father, reasonably enough, was extremely angry. He fetched me a stunning clout across the side of the head that would not have shamed Betty and demanded to know what the hell I thought I was playing at. My garbled apology/explanation, even when backed up by Daphne's sworn testimony, did not succeed in convincing him that the trap had not been intended for him.

The second incident occurred two days later. I had brought back a kite with me from Walton and was flying it in the meadow at the back of The Oaks when the string broke. I set off at top speed after it, tripped over a tangle of long grass, and hurtled headlong into a barbed wire fence. One strand caught me across the mouth; a rusty barb pierced my upper lip breaking one tooth and knocking loose another. Nevertheless, such was my determination to save my precious kite that I picked myself up, scrambled through the fence, and succeeded in catching hold of the trailing string just in time to prevent the kite from fluttering into a tree. Only then did I notice that my mouth was hurting abominably and that blood was trickling on to my shirt.

I was badly frightened; not, oddly enough, by my wound, but by the thought of what my father would say when he found out. After the bucket episode he had made it abundantly clear that he was thoroughly fed up with me and my silly tricks and that I had better mend my ways speedily or else . . . Having promised him tearfully that I would keep out of trouble, here I was up to my neck in it again.

I approached the house, taking good care not to be seen, and made my way into the deserted scullery. There I examined my face in a mirror. What I saw made me cry in real earnest and yet I still couldn't screw up the courage to go upstairs and tell my father what had happened. In the event he discovered me himself. He was not exactly overjoyed, but he wasn't as angry as I had expected he would be. He drove me into Colchester where the broken tooth was extracted and the loose one wired up. Luckily they were both first teeth.

My reaction on that occasion seems to me all of a piece with my nervous relationship with my father. He himself in his record of the incident speaks of "feelings of anger and indifference" towards me and, in an attempt to analyse the origin of them, confesses: "I often sense a sort of coldness and hostility in my attitude to Col, which is mysterious . . ." At least that entry suggests to me that in spite of the unfortunate bucket of water, I was not altogether without cause in detecting a certain ambiguity somewhere.

19

ON September 18th my father piled Mary, Ruby and myself, together with May and Daphne Deiner into the car and drove us all up to London. Our luggage had been loaded into the trailer which we towed along behind. Among the suitcases was one packed with the specified number of pairs of vests, pants, grey woollen stockings and grey flannel shirts that was ordained for pupils at Rendcomb College. These had been amassed for me and labelled with Cash's woven name tapes by May Deiner and Helen Deane.

The train from Paddington was due to leave at 1.55. My father lost the way and barely managed to get us there in time. Perhaps it was just as well. In the scurry and panic to get me aboard there was no time for protracted farewells. A brief kiss all round; a whistle shrilling; and I was on my way. I peered out of the smudged window and saw Mary gazing forlornly after me. She looked as depressed as I felt.

A boy even smaller than myself but twice as self-possessed was sitting opposite me. He had a pale, freckled face, sandy hair, a bright mauve cap and long trousers. He grinned at me and, rather tremulously, I grinned back. Whereupon he produced a slab of chocolate the size of a largish dictionary, broke off a chunk and offered it to me.

By the time we had reached Kemble Junction where we were to change trains, I had learnt, among other things, that his name was Austin James Caverhill, that his father was a doctor, that his ancestors were Scots, that he had recently been to America, and that he was going to be an orthopaedic surgeon.

In an effort to keep my end up I hinted that I had also been to America—I vaguely specified the Southern Continent—but was careful to add that I didn't remember much about it. I also let drop that my father owned a yacht. 'What does he do?' asked Caverhill.

'He writes books.'

'What sort of books?'

I clutched desperately. 'Books on Socialism.'

I'm glad he didn't ask me what that was.

At Kemble we found a group of older boys one of whom asked us if we were going to Rendcomb. When we admitted it he directed us across the platform to where another train was waiting. Having expected to be totally ignored or, at best, treated with lofty disdain, I was surprised by this apparent friendliness. Thretford had done nothing to eradicate the impression of boarding schools that *Tom Brown's Schooldays* had implanted within me. I could not conceive that Rendcomb might prove to be different in kind.

At Cirencester we were marshalled on to a bus and driven some five miles northwards along the Cheltenham road. As we passed a lodge house and a pair of tall wrought-iron gates a derisive groan went up. A mile or so further on we dipped down into a steep valley, passed a small cluster of grey, Cotswold stone houses and a village Post Office which evoked an ironic cheer, and then crossed a bridge over the river Churn. A couple of minutes later, having crawled in low gear up a four-in-one hill, we coasted down another drive, turned left on to an asphalted forecourt, and pulled up before a vast, pillared porch. Everyone scrambled out and the trunks and suitcases were unloaded from the luggage bay.

While I was waiting for my own to appear I looked around me. What I saw was a huge house, built of yellow Bath stone and dominated by a large, and remarkably ugly, square tower. On a broad windowsill some twenty feet above the ground two boys were perched, their legs dangling in air. They appeared to be playing chess. From a window even higher up another boy leaned out, whistled piercingly, and shouted a name. One of my fellow-travellers from the bus glanced up, cupped his hands to his mouth and bawled a greeting. Then a senior emerged on to the porch steps and shouted: 'Any new boys here?'

'Yes,' I said. 'Me.'

'And me,' echoed Caverhill.

'What are your names?'

We told him. He consulted a list in his hand; nodded; pencilled in a couple of ticks, and said: 'You're to report to the Head's study with your dog licences. This way.'

Caverhill and I lugged our suitcases into the outer hall, left them there and followed him into a gloomy inner hall which was dominated by a colossal marble statue of King Saul seated upon his throne. From there we trotted along yet another hall where we found ourselves tagged on to the end of a small queue of boys waiting outside a door labelled 'Headmaster's Study'. I observed that the others were all holding pieces of paper. 'What are those?' I whispered to Caverhill.

He put his hand into his inside pocket and produced an envelope. 'Health Certificate.'

'What's that?'

'To prove we haven't been in contact with any infectious disease. Where's yours?'

'I—I don't know.'

One or two of the others in the queue, hearing this, looked round at me curiously. One grinned and said: 'Watch out! He's got leprosy.' Another chanted: 'Unclean! Unclean!' and made believe he was ringing a bell.

Then the study door opened, a boy came out, and a brisk voice from within called: 'Next!'

The queue shuffled forward.

'They'll put you in Sick Bay, I expect,' observed Caverhill with all the suave assurance of a future orthopaedic surgeon.

'Disinfect him, you mean,' said the bell-ringer.

'Have you looked in your case?' suggested another helpfully. 'Maybe your Mum put it in there.'

I left the queue and ran back into the outer hall. The suitcases had all vanished! I felt as if I were drowning. Rushing through into the inner hall I cannoned into an immensely tall man who was coming the other way. 'Hey!' he cried, catching hold of me by the arm. 'What's the rush, tiddler?'

'My suitcase!' I gasped. 'I can't find it! It's gone!'

'Full of gold bullion, is it?'

I shook my head. 'My Health Certificate. I've got to find it.'

'Oh, is that all? Well, why don't you try your dormitory?'

'Where's that?'

He contemplated me for a moment and then grinned. 'Come on,' he said. 'What's your name?'

I told him.

He strode beside me back down the hall past the rapidly diminishing queue and led me up to a notice-board on which a list of names had been typed against the numbers of dormitories. He ran his finger down it until he found 'MURRY'. 'Last one on the top floor,' he sighed. 'It would be.'

He conducted me at great speed up flight after flight of stairs and down innumerable coconut-matted corridors till we reached a door on which was pinned a typewritten card bearing seven names, mine among them. He opened the door and we looked in. There, standing at the foot of one of the white iron beds was my missing suitcase. I flung myself upon it, wrenched it open, and saw lying on the top of my clothes a foolscap envelope. It was addressed, in my father's handwriting, to 'D. W. Lee-Browne Esq., Headmaster.'

The clouds rolled away; the sun came out; and all the birds in the world burst into song. 'Oh, *thank* you, sir,' I breathed, turning to my guide and comforter.

He laughed. 'Can you find your own way down again?'

'Oh, yes, sir. I think so.'

'You needn't call me "sir", you know. I'm not a member of staff.'

Grandpa, Grandma, J.M.M. and Mary at Larling

Outside the front door, the Old Rectory. Left to right from the back: Jimmy Young, Max Plowman, J. Hampden Jackson, Mary Horsfall (standing) Helen Young, Dorothy Plowman, J.M.M., Barbara Young, Virginia Young, Piers Plowman, Col, Weg

Granny Burlingham, Col and Mary, 1932

'Oh,' I said. 'Aren't you? What are you?'

'I'm a prefect.'

I was simply stunned. That a prefect should have gone out of his way to help me was beyond credence. Truly this school was proving to be unlike any I had ever imagined.

I found my own way back to the Headmaster's study. The queue had now disappeared altogether. I knocked on the door, twisted the handle and edged my way in. 'Why, hello, John!' cried a cheerful voice. 'Last but not least, eh? Where did you get to?'

I gaped at the man behind the desk. 'It's *you*!' I gulped.

My obvious astonishment made him chuckle. 'Come on,' he said, reaching out for my envelope. 'Let's see if you've brought us the Black Death from Essex.'

While he was reading the letter which my father had enclosed with my health certificate I tried to fit things together. I had last met this man at Larling a year before when he had driven over from Rockland St Peter with Jimmy Young. He had strolled out into the meadow where I was pitching a tent and had been surprisingly knowledgeable about a number of unexpected things, among them how to construct a camping oven out of two bricks and a biscuit tin covered with turf. I tried this out on my own after he left and it really worked. Now here he was sitting behind the headmaster's desk in my new school, a solid, chunky-looking man, with tufts of whisker on the tops of his cheeks, dark hair *en brosse*, and very blue and twinkling eyes.

'You had a good time on the Broads, I gather.'

'Yes, sir,' I said.

'And how do you like living at The Adelphi Centre?'

'It's all right.'

'But you prefer Larling, eh?'

I nodded.

Outside the door a bell began to jangle. The Head pushed back his leather-bound cuff and consulted the wrist watch which he wore strapped to the inside of his wrist. 'Tea time,' he said. 'Have you met the rest of your form yet?'

'Only Austin Caverhill, sir.'

'Well, you'll see the others in a minute.' He heaved himself out of his chair, came round to my side of the desk and offered me his hand. 'You're bound to have some ups and downs here,' he said, giving me a thoughtful look. 'I want you to promise me that if the downs ever get *really* deep you'll come and talk to me about it. All right?'

'Yes, sir.'

'I mean that, John,' he said. 'Or should we call you "Karl"?'

'John, sir.'

He nodded and released my hand. 'You'll do all right,' he said.

20

IT has sometimes occurred to me that if I had been able to go straight from my little school at Brighton to Rendcomb my life might well have been very different. Thretford, coming when it did and being what it was, numbed some growing point in me; convinced me that I was no good; reinforced my already profound sense of insecurity. It was to take the better part of five years to work myself free of the mental shackles which Reggie and Mr G— had imposed on me. That I was eventually able to do so was very largely due to the sympathy and understanding I received from D. W. Lee-Browne.

Rendcomb College was—and probably still is—an oddity among schools. It was founded in 1920 by the Wills family and heavily endowed from their tobacco fortune. The majority of the pupils were on full scholarships. These were all confined to the County of Gloucestershire. Once a year the eleven year old boys of the county were winnowed out and the brightest of them assembled in the Shire Hall in Gloucester where they sat an examination. The eight or ten thus selected became that year's basic intake for Rendcomb. Once their son had been accepted his parents had no further financial worries about his schooling. Everything, including pocket money, was provided and, at a stroke, social divisions within the school were eliminated. Furthermore, the staff/pupil ratio was such as to make any teacher in the average secondary school burst into tears. In my day the largest class at Rendcomb never held more than fifteen pupils, while in the sixth forms the average was half a dozen per subject. The prospect of teaching small classes of hand-picked highly intelligent pupils attracted an extremely gifted staff and it is hardly surprising that for many years Rendcomb's ratio of Open University Scholarships to pupils was among the highest in the country.

Had this been all the school offered it would not perhaps have differed very much from some of the intellectual forcing houses that are to be found in other countries—notably the Soviet Union. In fact Rendcomb was very different. It offered an education in practical democracy. The social life of the school was largely organized and run by the pupils themselves. The academic staff were to a considerable extent left free to concentrate upon their teaching. The basic organ of social government was the General Meeting which could be said to correspond roughly to the Lower House in the British Parliament. Every term elections were held for various offices and committees. The most important of these was the Council which consisted of seven members, all of whom were, as far as I remember, sixth formers. The Council had the power to punish members of the General Meeting who had infringed the rules or misbehaved themselves in other ways. If a boy felt he was being unfairly treated he was at liberty to bring his case up before the Council who would listen to the arguments for Prosecution and Defence, consult among themselves, and pass judgement accordingly. One was soon made aware both of the importance of an individual's rights within a society and the necessity, on occasion, of making those rights subservient to the needs of the society as a whole.

Very occasionally a conflict arose between the General Meeting and the authority of the school as represented by the

Headmaster, the academic staff, and the prefects—all of whom were appointed by the Head. These tussles were exciting while they lasted. Usually they ended in some amicable compromise being reached. If this proved impossible then the Headmaster reluctantly cracked his whip and everybody grumbled that it was just a sham democracy after all. In fact it wasn't, because within the ordained limits of the system, the power exercised by the Council and the General Meeting was real enough, and the members acquired a genuine sense of social responsibility as well as an appreciation of human values.

As new boys and members of Form I we were not immediately enfranchised. We were, however, expected to attend the Sunday morning General Meetings as silent observers. I found these rather boring and would have much preferred to be outside exploring the hundreds of acres of Cotswold wood, parkland and lake which made up the College grounds.

We also found ourselves grouped into Houses. There were three of these—East, West and South—and I was put in South. Every third week yours was Duty House and your House Prefects delegated the social duties for the week. These included helping to clean out the classrooms before breakfast, serving and clearing away in the dining hall, and being responsible for seeing that the bells were rung on time. Needless to say every boy was responsible for making his own bed and cleaning his own shoes.

One of the first lessons we learned was to respect public property. We thus became practical 'environmentalists' without realizing it, which is certainly the best way. A boy in the form immediately above mine was brought up before the Council for scattering orange peel in a flowerbed. He defended himself ingeniously on the grounds that his grandfather had told him that orange peel was good for roses and he had therefore been doing a public service. The Council was amused but unconvinced and sentenced him to pick up litter on two free afternoons.

Gradually the strangeness of the new surroundings wore off and I began to come to terms with Rendcomb. I was neither happy nor unhappy. In lessons I was soon outdistanced by the bright scholars but, apart from Latin which I loathed, I never fell so far behind as to drop right out of sight. At Art and Woodwork I was, indeed, among the best, and I shone at P.T. and games. But I made no really close friends, much as I should have liked to. It was not that I was an out and out isolate—there were remarkably few of those at Rendcomb—but simply that something in me cautioned me to withdraw a vital part of myself from contact with others. Possibly it was the old instinctive fear of being rejected.

My worst fault was that I was always losing things—books; items of clothing; pens and pencils. And I was incorrigibly untidy. Most of my form-mates contrived to keep their desks neat and shipshape but mine was inevitably a chaotic jumble. But pens were my real nightmare! They squeaked; they leaked; they fell on the floor and broke; they were bandaged and splinted until they didn't look like pens at all. By the end of my first term I had acquired a collection of bits and pieces which half-filled a fair sized cigarette tin, and I was well on the way to becoming a leading authority on the mechanism of the fountain pen. Even so it was to be years before I owned one which really worked consistently. By the end of prep each evening I usually looked as if I had been painting myself with woad.

The two members of staff I was eventually to get to know best were R. N. D. Wilson who taught English, and H. V. Molineaux who taught Art. Robin Wilson was an Irishman—specifically a Dubliner—a classicist and a man of wide culture. In appearance he looked rather like Hugh Lofting's portraits of his own 'Doctor Dolittle'. He had a blobby nose, a somewhat florid complexion, and a figure that, as he himself remarked, was built more for comfort than for speed. He was a most delightful person with a sly sense of humour and a genuine love of literature and art, but it was not until I eventually reached the sixth form that I came to appreciate his true worth.

Much the same goes for 'Molly' Molineaux. As juniors we were distinctly in awe of him. He was strict and rather gruff in manner, and with his clipped moustache and iron-grey hair had a decidedly forbidding military look about him. But his manner was but a protective veneer and, when I got to know him better and he had discerned that I had some talent, he became a very real friend and allowed me to appreciate the iconoclast who dwelt behind those cool grey eyes of his.

What principally distinguished Robin and Molly from the other members of the staff was that their perspectives were subtly different. In conversation with them one soon became aware that their spiritual horizons lay far beyond the walls of the school. Perhaps this was also true of some of the others but, if so, they did not succeed in communicating it to me. Though J. C. James the historian was probably the most brilliant and exciting *teacher* I have ever encountered I felt in some indefinable way that he was fulfilled in being what he was. The same was true to a certain extent of the biologist E. G. Neal, though as he has since made a name for himself as a leading world authority on badgers, I doubtless misjudged him.

I had been at Rendcomb for about a fortnight when a dark, curly-haired third former called Dobbs came up to me in the changing room one afternoon and said with a friendly grin: 'So you're from South America too. What part?'

For a moment I thought he must be pulling my leg and then, as though it were just happening, I saw myself facing Austin Caverhill across the train carriage spinning the tissue of bright lies to clothe my wilting ego. I gulped. 'Oh well,' I said weakly. 'It was a long time ago. I was just a baby really.'

'Were you born out there?'

'N-no,' I stammered. 'I was taken there. By my mother.'

He nodded. 'There were some Murrays at Valcheta. I thought maybe you were one of them.'

'Where's that?'

'Rio Negro. South Argentine.'

'Is that where you live?'

'We used to. We've moved to Buenos Aires now.'

'Oh,' I said.

He grinned again, said something to me in Spanish, and

sauntered off flicking his towel so that it cracked like a ring-master's whip.

For all the rest of that day I felt sick at heart, trapped within the web of my own stupid and pointless lie. I would succeed in forgetting it for a few minutes and then suddenly remember it again and feel worse than ever. That evening Robin Wilson happened to be supervising Junior Prep. Just before the bell was due to go for supper he beckoned me up to his desk. 'I've just been writing a letter to your father, John,' he said. 'Now what address shall I send it to?'

I stared at him aghast. I was quite certain that he had written to ask my father whether I had ever been in South America. At that moment the bell rang. There was an immediate shuffling of desks and chairs in the Big School. Mr Wilson called everyone to silence and then told them that they could go. He screwed the cap back on to his fountain pen and put it away in his pocket. 'You can let me have it in class tomorrow,' he said. 'There's no hurry. Now run along and wash that ink off your hands.'

I felt so wretched I could hardly eat my supper, and after supper I felt even worse. I had previously been looking forward to joining in a paper-pellet fight in the Big School which had been planned for that evening, but now I felt incapable of even stretching an elastic band let alone aiming a pellet. I wandered dismally out of the dining room, down the corridor past the lockers and round into the inner hall where the vast statue of King Saul brooded greyly. I laid a hand furtively on the cold marble toes and traced the relief of the stone sandal with my fingertip. "If the downs ever get *really* deep . . ." whispered a voice within my head. How deep was "really deep"? No need to ask—I knew. Turning on my heel I trailed slowly down the main hall, drew a deep breath and knocked on the Headmaster's door. As I heard his voice say 'Come in', incontinently I burst into tears.

I wonder what Lee-Browne made of the small and inky figure who crept weeping round his study door? For my own part I have only the haziest recollection of that interview which, by some inexplicable detour, ended up with us talking about Jimmy Young. My lie had somehow diminished from a mountain to a molehill. He made me promise that I'd tell Austin Caverhill the truth by myself; as for Mr Wilson and Dobbs I wasn't to worry. As I was making my way out he called me back, pulled open a drawer in his desk and handed me three large elastic bands. 'You've still got half an hour left,' he said. 'Good shooting.'

A minute or so later I wriggled my way in behind the barricade of desks and chairs that spanned one end of the Big School and sought out Caverhill. I crouched down beside him and began sniping at the enemy. During a brief lull in the battle I blurted out my confession to him. He looked a bit surprised and then he grinned. 'And what about the yacht?'

I flushed and swallowed hard. 'We hired it from Wroxham.'

A well-aimed pellet zipped through the palisade and stung my cheek like a wasp.

'That's Hatherall,' growled Caverhill. 'I'll get the bastard.'

The ordeal was over.

21

TOWARDS the end of October I received a letter from my father. I was astonished to see that the address he gave was 'The Old Rectory, Larling'. The postmark confirmed it. The letter was very brief. In it he told me that he had heard from Mr Wilson that I was settling in well and that he and Bodge had just bought a Welsh pony called 'Taffy' for young Mary. He ended with the words: 'Betty sends you her love.'

When I had got over my initial surprise I discovered that I was pleased. Fond as I was of Helen Deane and the people at the Centre there was no doubt at all in my mind that Larling was my real home. I had no idea of *how* the reconciliation had been brought about and, knowing Betty, I could not believe it would be permanent, but in those days I lived almost wholly in the present. As I saw it, Weg, Mary and I would be together again with Bodge and Rue, and I would go fishing and rabbiting with Gordon. I asked nothing better of life.

Some thirty-five years were to pass before I even began to comprehend the true nature of the spiritual crisis which lay behind that letter of my father's. His actions at this time drove his friends to despair and delighted his enemies. Richard Rees roundly pronounced him mad; Max Plowman sighed; Helen Young wept. And all, in their own terms, were justified. But their terms were not his and, in the last resort, their need of him was greater than his of them.

The cable which my father had sent to Helen in June had brought her to Southampton on *The Bremen* at the end of September. There he met her and they went to an hotel at Lymington where they spent the next three days. What they learned about themselves and each other during those three days I can only guess at, but by the end of them my father noted in his journal "I feel as though I had entered on a veritable waste-land." I daresay Helen must have felt the same. What she needed from him he was incapable of giving her; what he needed, she averred, no woman on earth was capable of giving him. He foresaw in their relation "an interminable and exhausting claim upon me, which I could never satisfy except at the cost of my own integrity". In short he had learnt that she wanted him to be something he was not. Was it a father or a god? I doubt whether either of them ever knew.

I think it was Helen who first faced up to the bitter truth that they had both been deluding themselves, but then she was a pessimist where love was concerned and he was an optimist. Nevertheless, within seven days of their arrival at Langham it was apparent to them both that there was no real future in their relationship. Yet, as my father had once observed of himself: "Love something or someone I must." In his own way, at least as much as she in hers, he needed the nourishment and security of love if he was to live at all. But, such was his nature, he could not pay for love at the price of his own integrity, by which he meant "not suffering the fine point of the soul to be blunted, not permitting any self-violation, not acquiescing in any profound inner division". To love Helen as she demanded would have meant all those things and, most telling of all, it would have meant abandoning young Mary. By October 14th the brief and agonizing struggle was over and he had emerged, as he put it, "into a strange condition of absolute sorrow and joy . . . a *vita nuova*". The next day he returned to Larling and to Betty.

I suspect that the only person in the world who, knowing all the circumstances, sincerely believed that he was doing the right thing, was my father himself. Helen prophesied grimly that 'the next few years will be a bloodier Hell than anything I ever saw at Larling'; Betty, once she was assured that her triumph over 'that fucking whore' was absolute, rounded on my father and berated him for not realizing that all women were bitches; even his brother Richard, the most loyal of all his supporters, was baffled and dismayed. My father would have none of it. He *knew*. Having read the unpublished sequel to *Between Two Worlds* which he wrote at this time I am reminded of nothing so much as the barely coherent ecstasy of a condemned prisoner who, at the last possible second, has been reprieved from the firing squad. He would have been justified in adapting Lawrence's title and calling it *But Look! I Have Come Through*. The question still to be answered was—through to what?

Well, in the first instance, through to Pacifism. On the very same day that he returned to Larling and to Betty he had joined Dick Sheppard's 'Peace Pledge Union'. Max Plowman, naturally, was overjoyed; but the members of The Adelphi Centre who had been prepared to march alongside my father in his crusade under the banner of Militant Socialism were outraged. My father who had discovered—or rediscovered—that "Love is God" and had "proved it on his pulses" was surprised but relatively unperturbed by the consternation which the news of his latest conversion produced among his followers. As he remarked to me many years later with a wry smile: 'True, I have incessantly been mistaken. But since I have tried to keep myself open to experience, my mistakes haven't worried me: I have been able to accept them as minor revelations.'

The point about my father's 'mistakes' was that they *were* all his own. At one time or another every one of his friends must have warned him of some terrible and gaping pitfall that he was heading straight towards. Blandly he proceeded and, sure enough, he tumbled straight into it. When his friends removed their hands from before their eyes it was to view with astonishment his dogged and battered figure drag itself up from the depths, shake its head, and straightaway beetle off in a totally unexpected direction.

The deepest pit of them all—one so profound, indeed, that none but he himself ever plumbed it to its uttermost depths—was his second attempt to make a go of his marriage to Betty. Within a matter of weeks of the reconciliation he had begun to realize that, though he himself might have changed, she had not. What is more, in 'betraying' her with Helen he had handed her a club with which to beat him. What had led up to that betrayal in the first place did not concern her: she had been 'wronged' and he was going to be made to pay for it. The fury which was eventually to be unleashed at The Old Rectory was something so dark and elemental it is beyond my powers to describe. I find that I lack any scale of normal human experience upon which to draw for reference. Only once did I ever come across anything that seemed in any way remotely like it, and that was in a court case report in *The News of the World* in which the defendant, goaded ultimately beyond the limits of human endurance, had snatched up a hammer and battered his terrible tormentor into the ultimate silence of death.

To those who will doubtless say: 'Well, why didn't he leave her then?' I can only reply: 'Because he wouldn't have been himself if he had.' So long as even the tiniest spark of love for Betty existed within him he could not deny its claim upon him. To have done so would have been to deny the truth of that moment of illumination with Helen—the overwhelming revelation that "Love is God". And always and above all there was Mary; a living proof of the love he had felt for her mother and which, he believed, he was feeling again.

So confident was he in the dawn of the new era that he insisted that Betty must have another child who would be a living witness to the validity of their reconciliation and to the ultimate triumph of love. She was happy enough to acquiesce, though I doubt whether her reasons matched his own. To her another child simply meant that my father would be chained even more securely to Larling and to herself. As it transpired nearly a year was to pass before David was begotten and, in spite of my father's high hopes, few children can ever have had a less auspicious conception.

22

HAVING decided to my own satisfaction that I would be spending the Christmas holiday at Larling I was disappointed (though not altogether surprised) to find that I was to spend it at the Centre after all. Weg was still in Belgium—temporarily out of harm's way—and, since my father would be occupied with the Christmas Conference, it seemed sensible to him that we should all be at Langham with him. 'All' naturally now included Betty, Mary and Ruby.

Among the newcomers at the Centre I discovered a pale and extremely pretty girl called Joan Easedale. I found her attractive but a bit mystifying. She seemed to do everything in slow-motion, and for a lot of the time she just sat and read books in a deck-chair in the conservatory with a rug over her knees. She had a gift of persuading people to talk about themselves. I cannot recall her ever volunteering much information on her own account, but she did once tell me that she wanted to be a writer. Since about half the people I had met at the

Centre seemed to have similar ambitions this did not strike me as being in any way remarkable.

One day she got me talking about Thretford and I told her about Reggie. Either inadvertently or because I wanted to see how she would react (I suspect now that it was the latter) I let drop a casual remark about Reggie and Stubbo's sessions in the bog. Miss Easedale's eyes widened perceptibly and a bright flush crept all the way up her neck to the tips of her cheeks. 'They did *what*?' she whispered.

I repeated it word for word and then enquired guilelessly: 'Don't they do things like that at girls' schools?'

Miss Easedale shuddered and made haste to divert the conversation into less horrific channels, during which I seem to remember her telling me that her favourite story was *The Secret Garden* by Frances Hodgson Burnett.

My Christmas present that year was a B.S.A. air rifle. The compression spring was so powerful that I had to rest the butt on the ground and 'break' the weapon with both hands in order to load it. Furthermore I was so small that I had to tuck the stock in *under* my arm in order to take aim. Even so, within a day or two I had become a very fair shot and I could hardly wait to get my prize back to Larling and to show it off to Gordon. My father, hoping perhaps to instil into me a modicum of caution, rationed me initially to a dozen lead pellets a day. I found this so frustrating that I begged two shillings from Rue and persuaded Butling to buy me a secret supply in Colchester.

It may seem strange that anyone so publicly wedded to the cause of non-violence as my father was should have encouraged his son in the use of firearms. In fact my father greatly enjoyed shooting and Larling was over-run with rabbits. More than once I had been awakened in the early hours of the morning by a shattering report from the bedroom next door. It was only my father taking a pot-shot at a rabbit out of the window with a 4.10. His record for one week was six rabbits with eight shots. Luckily we all liked rabbit stew.

The Christmas Conference ended with a party which I

enjoyed enormously. Max Plowman contributed a barrel of strong cider which he tapped and placed in the conservatory. I had never sampled cider before and that evening, when no one was about, I slipped into the conservatory and helped myself liberally. Some fifteen or twenty minutes later I found myself standing on a table 'taking off' various guests. It was the old 'giddy goat' act and it brought the house down. It also brought my father down. He came into the room with Betty just at the very moment when I was fairly launched into my 'Middleton Murry' imitation. I caught sight of him and promptly fell off the table. I doubt whether Charlie Chaplin could have bettered it for timing, and I was told afterwards that Max Plowman laughed so much he gave himself a severe stitch. I was ushered ignominiously upstairs, undressed and put to bed. Next morning I had a hangover.

That same day we returned to Larling. During the drive from Langham Betty kept up a nagging refrain about 'that bitch'—the mildest of her epithets for Helen Young—and accused my father of making passes at Helen Deane and Joan Easedale. His response was to return the soft answer which is supposed to turn aside wrath. If anything it did just the opposite. By the time we reached the Old Rectory I knew for a certainty that not only had nothing changed but that nothing ever *would* change. I was right.

No sooner was I back at school than I succumbed to some mysterious germ and retired to Sick Bay with a raging temperature. After I had been in bed for nearly three weeks the Headmaster decided I was malingering and told Matron to get me back into circulation. She did so under protest. Two days later I was back in again with a record 104°. This time no one needed convincing that I really was ill. I was removed from the Sick Bay, put into the Guest Room, and given V.I.P. treatment, though to start with I felt so wretched I didn't fully appreciate it.

One night I woke up convinced that I was about to die. I was soaked with sweat and could feel something squatting on my chest. It seemed like an enormous toad. I knew that at any second it would shuffle up on to my face and suffocate me. I tried to push it away but my arms refused to move. I tried to call out for help but the only sound I could produce was a sort of wheezy croak. For the second time in my life I knew the meaning of terror. It was Grimes Graves all over again only infinitely worse, because this time there was no hope of escape. Then, just as I was about to give up, I became aware of an extraordinary, high-pitched, singing sound. It seemed to be coming from right inside my ear, minute and clear, like an insect trapped in the throat of a flower. One moment it was near; the next, far, far away; but it was always *there* and, listening to it, I gradually forgot my fear and knew that I had been allowed another chance. From that moment on I began to get well again.

As I regained my strength I discovered that among the advantages of my isolation was that the maids used to clean the room, bring me my meals and tidy up my bed. One of them I grew particularly fond of. She had a sweet face, dark, coppery-red hair, tawny eyes and a beautiful creamy complexion. One day, to my surprise and delight, as she bent over to straighten up my pillows, she kissed me. The ardour with which I responded must have surprised her. 'You're a saucy one and no mistake,' she laughed. 'I thought you were supposed to be ill.'

'I am,' I said, catching hold of her hand. 'Feel my heart. I think it's stopped beating.'

She allowed me to guide her hand inside my pyjama jacket. 'Stopped?' she said. 'Don't you believe it! It's going like a train.'

'How about yours?' I asked, and before she could stop me I had my hand on one of her breasts.

She let it stay there for a moment then drew back and eyed me quizzically. '*How* old did you say you were?'

'Twelve,' I lied.

She shook her head, though whether in disbelief or astonishment I did not know. Then she gave me a thoughtful little smile and went out.

Matron herself brought me my lunch and I had given up hope of seeing my favourite again that day when, to my inexpressible delight, she appeared with my tea. As she set it down on the bedside table I caught hold of her wrist and pulled her down on to the side of my bed. 'Hey, what are you up to?' she whispered.

'Seeing if your heart's beating.'

'Well? Is it?'

I slipped my hand in behind the barricade of her starched apron and felt the astonishing fullness of her young breast. Purely instinctive I ducked my head and kissed her through the green cloth of her tunic. She brought her arms round and pressed me briefly to her. 'Is it?' she murmured. 'Is it?'

At the risk of disappointing anyone who may read this, I might as well say here and now that that was as far as it ever went. Yet, slight as the incident was, it has remained with me ever since as something wholly precious. Perhaps for that very reason I never built it up into a sexual fantasy to impress my friends. Indeed, I never mentioned it to them at all; but I often thought about it, and when I did my feelings were always of a most gentle gratitude.

By the time I was finally pronounced to be well again the term was almost half over and I had dropped way behind the rest of my class. As far as Latin was concerned the lapse proved fatal. Whereas before I had just managed to stagger along a barely discernible track, now I was lost in an impenetrable jungle of unknown declensions and meaningless constructions. In an effort to bring me up with the rest, Mr Gross the Latin master set me to learn by heart all the things I had missed, whereupon, to my utter dismay, I discovered that my gift for rapid memorizing had completely deserted me. Now I was lost indeed; nor was I helped by my realization that Mr Gross was at least as bewildered as I was. What made perfect sense to him obviously made none at all to me. Patiently he explained it all over again, but his words seemed to dissolve around me and I was swirled away down the plughole of total incomprehension. In the end I simply gave up and burst into tears.

In his report on my progress at the end of term Mr Gross gave it as his opinion that I was having difficulty in making up lost ground. My father read this and decided he would lend Mr Gross a helping hand. After all, with a Double First in Oxford Classical Mods and a host of prize medals of one sort and another for Latin and Greek, he no doubt reasoned that *Latin for Today* should present no problems to any child of his. He was mistaken. I just could not see the *point* of it at all. My daily tutorials with him became an absolute agony of spirit, and during that holiday I think I came as near to hating him and myself and Latin and the whole bloody nonsensical English educational system as I was ever to do in all the rest of my life. Certainly at the end of that grim four weeks we had built up between us an all but impenetrable wall of non-communication—a barrier which, though it was to be breached occasionally in the years ahead, was never again to be wholly demolished.

Latin lessons with my father were not the only innovation to be introduced into Larling in the spring of 1937. While I was away at school he had been re-thinking his own situation *vis-à-vis* the Church. The need to do this had sprung directly out of his conversion to Pacifism, but its roots lay, I suspect, far back in his own past and in his just evaluation of himself as a social *déraciné*. The more deeply he read back into English social history the more he became convinced that the great flaw in the Reformation lay in the break-down of the village commune for which the Mediaeval Church had been both the symbol and the focus of social integration. He determined that any further experiment he might eventually make in communal living should be based on a return to the land. Meanwhile, was it not possible that a spiritual revival could be kindled among the dry tinder of the disintegrating Socialist movement? Once again he set out to prove it upon his pulses. Early in 1937 he resumed his church-going, and began to toy with the idea of taking Holy Orders.

The stumbling block here was, of course, Betty. How could he hope to convert anyone of his view of a Christian Socialist Utopia when his own marriage was such a mockery of everything a Christian marriage was supposed to be? Very well then, by means of love and gentleness and understanding he would endeavour to lead his wife to a belief in God. It was, I sincerely believe, the most heroic task he ever attempted; and though it failed, and in the end failed miserably, even its failure deserved to be accounted, in its own way, as a sort of triumph.

The first signs I saw of the new regime were at breakfast on the first morning of the Easter Holidays. I had just taken my place at table and was looking forward to dribbling golden-syrup patterns over my porridge, when I saw my father open a black, leather-covered book and slip a book marker out of it. I glanced round at Betty and she frowned at me, shook her head and looked demurely down at her lap. Rue tiptoed in and stood with eyes downcast in the doorway. Even young Mary put on a wholly unnatural, pious expression which made me want to kick her. A moment later my father cleared his throat and began to read from the Psalms.

The reading did not last longer than a couple of minutes. He closed up the book, murmured something about 'In the name of Our Lord Jesus Christ . . .' and everyone intoned 'Amen'. I felt a terrible nervous compulsion to giggle but, luckily, I managed to control it. Betty started ladling out the porridge and my father restored the prayer book to its place on the shelf and began to open his letters.

By the end of the holiday the breakfast service had lengthened by two Psalms to five minutes. It seemed to me that Betty was getting a bit restless but, remarkable to relate, there had been no violent outburst. Not at breakfast anyway, and I had long since grown accustomed to the dreary obscene litany I heard almost nightly through my bedroom wall. Was it possible that I had been wrong after all and that things were gradually going to get better? I suggested as much to Rue but she merely observed that leopards didn't change their spots however many prayers you said. So I went my own way as usual and, in the blessed intervals between wrestling with *Latin for Today*, I shot my first rabbit with my new air-rifle and constructed a house high up in a tree for Mary and myself.

23

WITH the evergreen exception of Greyfern, and in spite of Latin, my first summer at Rendcomb was the happiest term I had spent in any school. Early in May a craze for constructing model aeroplanes broke out like an epidemic and in an attempt to confine the resultant mess within manageable limits a room was set aside and designated as the Hobbies Room. I signed on as a junior aero-modeller and spent much of my spare time constructing gliders and rubber-powered 'duration' models out of balsa wood and tissue paper. My machines tended to lack finish because I was always in such a tearing hurry to get them into the air, but I did have a knack of flying them successfully which was denied to some of the others. I thus carved out another small but precious toe-hold for my self-esteem.

If I had devoted to my lessons one tenth of the energy I expended upon such extra-curricular activities my academic record might have made less depressing reading. In the examination lists at the end of term my name was usually found nearer the bottom than the top, though I did surprise myself by coming second in History. I did not, alas, surprise either myself or Mr Gross by coming bottom in Latin. Being a generous man by nature he awarded me 5%, which included one mark for imagination. Having spotted the name 'Polyphemus' in the passage set for unseen translation I staked all on a single desperate throw and gave him the whole hair-raising episode of Ulysses in the Cyclops' cave, plus sheep, plus 'Noman', plus the blinding of the giant. Unfortunately it either wasn't that 'Polyphemus' or was but a passing reference to him. Even so I think I earned my single mark. What the other 4% was for I can't imagine.

The realization that by my dismal performance I had condemned myself to another holiday of lessons with my father did not depress me as much as might have been expected. I had only to be away from Larling for a month or so for it to acquire in my mind's eye a blessèd, hazy autumnal glow. I remembered all I loved about the place and simply ignored what I hated. As a result I would arrive home from school bubbling over with schemes for my own and my sisters' diversion. For a while my enthusiasm would carry all before it as I organized camps in the woods, constructed fire-balloons, planned bow and arrow raids on Mr Lumley's long-suffering chickens. It was all so intense, so frenetic, that it could not last. Nor did it. Sooner or later I would overreach myself and retribution would descend. Usually it took the form of Betty, but not always. One memorable exception was 'The Great Taffy Ambush'.

Having failed in numerous attempts to ride the pony who, wise in her fashion, would never allow us to get anywhere near her, I decided we would stalk her through the undergrowth with our bows and arrows. It worked after a fashion. As Weg, Mary and I rose whooping like Cherokees from the bushes, Taffy set off at a thunderous gallop, mane and tail streaming, with our reed arrows skimming vainly in pursuit. My father, disturbed at his work, emerged wrathfully from his study and read us the Riot Act. We listened sheepishly then sloped off into the walled garden and busied ourselves about some less obvious devilry.

Ten minutes later we heard a stern shout of: 'Col! Weg!' and eyed each other apprehensively. Next moment my father strode into the walled garden and, trembling with rage, accused us of tormenting Taffy after he had expressly forbidden us to do so.

Indignant and astonished I protested our innocence,

prudently ducking as he aimed a furious swipe at my head. Weg elected to stand her ground and collected a hefty box on the ear.

White faced she drew herself up, and fixing him with her luminous tear-filled eyes commanded: 'Hit me again, Dadda!'

It was magnificent! Boadicea and Joan of Arc rolled into one! My father quailed before her. He peered doubtfully at us both. 'You mean you *didn't* chase Taffy again?'

'I *told* you we didn't,' I said. 'You told us not to, didn't you?'

He looked from me back to Weg and from her received a look of such withering contempt that his toes must have curled.

Even so I did not care to push my luck too far. 'Come on,' I muttered to her. 'What's the use? He doesn't believe us.'

Superbly she turned her back on him and together we marched away.

That particular incident occurred, I believe, at the beginning of the summer holiday though it might well have been later, for when I arrived home at the end of July it was to find the Old Rectory turned upside down and a squad of ex-Centre people, led by my Uncle Richard, busily converting the old stables, the granary, and every possible attic and box-room into accommodation for the guests at the final Adelphi Summer School. On enquiry I was informed that the Centre at Langham had recently been taken over by Max Plowman and the P.P.U. as a home for Basque refugee children and so was no longer available.

No one worked harder at the preparations than Betty. When she was doing something she was good at and had no occasion to brood upon her deeply ingrained sense of inferiority she was another person altogether. If only she could always have been like it, how different our lives might have been!

Weg had turned up a few days before the Summer School was due to open. I had not seen her for over a year and was astonished at the change in her. She had grown several inches taller and spoke English with a marked French accent. She also kept mixing French words into English sentences, a practice which I found highly amusing. To start with we were oddly shy with one another but it soon wore off as we set about devising means of raising pocket money for our holidays.

The result of our labours was *The Red Star Gazette*. The name—a fortuitous stroke of brilliant opportunism—derived not from any particular Left Wing sympathies, but from the fact that we used a scarlet crayon when designing the cover. Nevertheless, when we brought out our first number, priced at an exhorbitant 3d, and placed it prominently among the piles of rather dreary pamphlets with titles like *Towards a New Jerusalem* and *Forward with Marx*, the Summer School guests snapped up our *Gazette* as though it were a collector's item. We hastened to produce six copies of No. 2. Each edition was limited to the number of legible impressions we could contrive with a pencil and carbon paper and, rapacious though we were, even we had serious doubts about the bottom copy. By the time we had No. 3 off the presses we had run out of both carbon paper and inspiration. If only we had had Daphne Deiner on our staff! Even so the editors cleared two shillings each and the office boy (Mary) sixpence, which put *The Red Star Gazette* in the best-seller class compared to *Forward with Marx*.

We enjoyed that Conference enormously. The weather was glorious and we made a host of new friends. Among them were two delightful young American students called Lucia and Elizabeth who seemed only too willing to be enticed away to play games with us in the woods when they ought by rights to have been attending lectures. Another was a young Cambridge undergraduate who, overcome with shyness, had turned tail and fled from the Conference only to be pursued and brought back by Betty. One morning Weg, Mary and I discovered him sitting peacefully reading in a deck-chair on the lawn and attacked him in line-astern with pea-shooters. He bore it stoically for a while then leapt up, pursued us, caught us, and stuffed dried grass down our necks. From this unlikely introduction was to spring a life-long friendship, for the young man in question was Frank Lea, later to become assistant editor of

The Adelphi and eventually the official biographer of my father.

On the day after the Summer School ended Betty reverted to her old self. I suppose the strain of keeping her temper for over a fortnight had simply proved too much for her. Unfortunately I happened to be directly in the firing line when it happened. She accused me of calling her a liar—something I would not have dared to do in a thousand years—and simply flew at me in front of the handful of guests who had remained behind. I don't suppose they had ever seen anything like it in their lives. Betty, possessed by her demon of annihilation, always had a strangely paralysing effect on those who witnessed the phenomenon for the first time. She had struck me hard several times about the head before someone thought to pull us apart. I fled howling and, as usual, sought sanctuary in the woods.

By an oversight my father's record of his response to this particular incident has escaped the censoring scissors. Louise Simon, one of the guests present, recounted to him what had happened and he, after noting the circumstances, commented: "It was a fearful *exhibition*. The only excuse is that B. is B. and that she was particularly tired. But it is no use thinking '*j'ai pris mon assiette*' and my only concern is that the children should not feel that any essential injustice is done to them. A blow in passion, however unjust, does not do any real harm; and my trust is that the children do feel that, in spite of all, B. is a *warm* human being: which she is. But—heavens above!—mine is a difficult life."

The question that entry poses is how does one evaluate 'real harm'? The sort of Christ-like detachment of 'Father, forgive them; for they know not what they do' is perfectly acceptable providing 'they' are doing it to 'you'. On this particular occasion I did not just *feel* that an essential injustice was being done to me I damn well *knew* it was! Multiply that incident by a hundredfold in my case and a thousandfold in Weg's and it is possible to grasp why we at least would have hesitated to endorse my father's opinion of Betty at that time as "a warm human being" and as "a queer, lovable, childish creature". While prepared to concede that I was prejudiced I also believe I had every right to be.

When I had recovered sufficiently to review the situation I crept back indoors, sought out Betty and begged her to forgive me. She did so, grudgingly, after first making me admit that I was in the wrong and had, in consequence, got no more than I deserved. I was only too willing to agree. Those who, at about this time, were being nonplussed by the "confessions" in the Soviet show-trials, would, by observing my behaviour, have discovered that confessing to a crime one had not committed was by no means the sole prerogative of Comrade Radek and his unfortunate associates. At one time or another Weg and I must have 'confessed' to enough infamy to have qualified us both for a sizable Borstal stretch. Only by grovelling in this way could we buy ourselves the precarious right to exist at all. Once incurred the pressure of Betty's prolonged wrath was such that a child simply could not withstand it. I am thus inclined to think that my father, in his deliberations, may have missed the crucial point. Enforced self-abasement of the kind to which my sister and I were subjected may well have proved far more damaging in the long run than any number of blows "struck in passion" by "a queer, lovable, childish creature".

Shortly after the Summer School ended we went for a week's holiday to Hemsby on the Norfolk coast. This time we camped. My father, for reasons connected with *The Adelphi*, did not come with us and the position of senior male in the *entourage* was taken by my Uncle Richard. Louise Simon and a friend completed the party. Up till then I had always regarded Richard with a certain degree of circumspection, not to say awe. I knew that he thought me cheeky—which I surely was—and he had his own effective but painful methods of putting me in my place when I overstepped the mark. Now, for the first time, I came to appreciate him as a person, and I discovered that I liked him enormously. When he chose he could be quite hysterically funny. Furthermore he seemed to have acquired a knack of handling Betty—pulling her leg and joshing her along—that my father signally lacked. As a result of his efforts Betty was never allowed to build up a lethal head of steam and the week passed all too quickly.

A few days after our arrival we learnt that certain public-spirited local inhabitants were organizing a children's fête in a field adjoining the beach. Races of various kinds were advertised and—supreme attraction!—cash prizes were to be awarded. There and then Weg and I decided to enter ourselves for everything. We even cajoled Mary into the Infants' section. We had left ourselves no time in which to practise but we were used to things like 'three-legged' and 'wheel-barrow' races, having experimented with them at Larling on many occasions.

In the event it became quite an embarrassing afternoon for our adults because Weg and I won every single race for which we were eligible to enter, even though, by the end of the session, we were being handicapped almost out of sight by the perspiring curate who was in charge. We left the field feeling like millionaires and thereafter basked in the unfamiliar, heady sensation of being pointed at on the beach by other less speedy children and whispered about to their parents.

By the time the holiday ended all my winnings were gone, frittered away in gambling on slot-machines, for which I had a passion, and on an extra-large kite. I returned to Larling penniless and promptly remembered all the things I ought to have done with my bonanza. One of these was to invest two shillings in the purchase of a Meccano 'Magic' clockwork motor. A boy in my form at school owned one and I had long coveted a similar machine. No sooner had I remembered this than I became obsessed by the desire to have one to take back to school with me. The problem, as always, was money.

On the face of it nothing would have been simpler than to go to my father and ask him for some. He would, I am sure, have listened patiently, sighed, then smiled and produced a two-shilling piece. I know that *now*. But in 1937 I could no more have *asked* him for money than I could have sprouted wings and flown. There were two reasons for this. Firstly, both Weg and I were convinced that my father was terribly hard up, literally down to his last few pounds. And not only Weg and I believed this. Once when he was departing for London, Mary produced her purse, which must have contained all of sixpence, and pressed it into his hand. My father was deeply touched by her act, as well he might have been, but only Weg and I knew *why* she had done it. She believed it would make the vital difference between a ham sandwich for him at Liverpool St station and no food at all. I don't really know why my father chose to foster this notion of his poverty among his children, perhaps it was wholly unintentional on his part, but there is no doubt that we believed it absolutely.

The second reason I could not ask him for the two bob—or anything else for that matter—was the old, deeply-rooted fear that he might say no. Such a rejection was something I simply dared not risk. But, oh God, how I wanted that clockwork motor!

When we got back from Hemsby, Uncle Richard was lent my room and I was put to sleep in the old nursery. This had done service as an office during the Summer School and there were still some odd bits and pieces of office stationery lying around. Most of this had been bundled into a big black and yellow tallboy. Nosing curiously through this cupboard one evening I discovered, pushed right to the back, a cardboard shoebox. I pulled it out and found it contained, besides miscellaneous odds and ends, a notebook labelled 'Postage' and a yellow cigarette tin. I prised open the tin. Inside were a few paperclips, some elastic bands, a couple of penny stamps, and coins to the value of two shillings and sevenpence halfpenny.

I don't think I hesitated at all. A shilling, a sixpence and the necessary assorted coppers were inside my trousers pocket before you could have said: 'From each according to his means'. I restored the shoebox to its place at the back of the cupboard, shut the door on it and, half an hour later, was bathed and in bed.

It was a long time before I fell asleep and, when I did, I was plagued with hideous nightmares. Fortunately I have forgotten the precise form they took but I clearly remember that large and remarkably hairy spiders played a prominent part in them. In my efforts to escape I woke myself up and lay there trembling in the darkness. I knew exactly what had caused the nightmares; knew that I had only to get out of bed, take the two shillings out of my trousers pocket and restore it to its rightful place in the yellow tin and all would be well.

I climbed out of bed, switched on the light and padded over to the cupboard with my loot. But my heart was heavy. Somewhere, I felt sure, there must exist an avenue of compromise which would both relieve my tortured conscience and still allow me to enjoy the fruits of my sin. As I groped for the shoebox, Lucifer himself took pity on me and slipped the 'Postage' notebook into my hand. It fell open at the very page which contained the final entry. I ran my eye down the column of figures and then—almost, I swear, of its own volition—a pencil had leapt between my fingers and was writing '*Sept 14th . . . to one Mecanno Magic Moter . . . 2/–*'. Five minutes later the box was back in its place, the cupboard shut, the light out. And Horatio Bottomley the second? He, it pains me to record, was sleeping the sleep that is supposed to reward the innocent and the just.

24

I ARRIVED back at Rendcomb to discover that a pale and rather podgy new boy had joined our form. I found him disconsolately eyeing one of the noticeboards and asked him who he was. He told me his name was Norman Stone and that he should by rights have come the previous year. He had a thin band of scarlet ribbon stitched round the sleeve of his grey flannel jacket to show that he had recently been vaccinated against smallpox and was therefore excused P.T. I guessed that he was feeling lost and that he didn't want anyone to suspect it, so I suggested casually that he might as well 'sit' with me for the time being and explained to him what this entailed. Every week we all changed places in the dining hall. Friends usually arranged to sit together in groups and these groups were circulated around the various tables. Each table was supervised by prefects and presided over by at least one member of the academic staff. A new 'table list' was made out each week by the Head Prefect and pinned to a noticeboard on Sunday evenings. Norman listened to my explanation, considered my offer carefully, and then agreed. Though I am sure neither of us could possibly have suspected it, he and I were destined to remain table-companions for the next six years.

Apart from sharing the same 'goonish' sense of humour we were an oddly assorted couple. Norman was short-sighted and rather clumsy but with a mind as quick as a dozen silverfish. In lessons he had the enviable ability to pick up things without appearing to pay the slightest attention to what his teachers were saying. Most of his time he spent scribbling cartoons in the margins of his notebooks and his desk was at least as untidy as my own. He was a voracious reader and he also had trouble with his fountain pens. In retrospect I think there was something extraordinarily precocious about him. As I had in Leslie Abbot, I recognized in Norman someone who was determined to dictate his own terms, and throughout his career at Rendcomb he did just that.

By the time we had both reached the sixth form he had already been singled out by J. C. James as a potential open scholarship candidate. Undoubtedly Norman could have walked off with such an honour in either French, English or History but he simply wasn't interested, or at least not sufficiently interested to do the amount of work required. During the term when he should have been poring over his text books he was teaching himself to play the trumpet. When the time came for him to sit for his scholarship he had prepared only one historical topic in any depth. His general essay was brilliant, but that, virtually, was the end of it. However, not wishing to waste the fruits of his erudition, he prefaced his English History paper with the following foreword: 'I see that you have omitted to ask a question on the "Enclosure System". I should not like to think that you had, by this oversight, deprived yourselves of the chance to hear my views upon this fascinating topic.' He then spent his three hours writing a fifteen page essay on the subject. I somehow doubt whether Mr James was as amused as I was when Norman told me what he had done.

But that was still far into the future. In 1937 it would have taken a truly inspired seer to divine the hidden potential in our form. Apart from one or two obvious academic high-flyers we were a decidedly nondescript bunch and were, on more than one occasion, corporately accused of lacking public spirit. Speaking for myself that Winter Term was the start of a thoroughly barren patch in my school career. It began with my being drummed out of the Puppeteers which I had joined in the previous Spring Term. The immediate cause of my dismissal was my using a male and a female marionette to stage a private 'blue show' for one or two other members of the team. A rather straitlaced senior happened to come in just when the action was at its height and I was reported to Mr Molineaux who lost no time in dispensing with my services. Some years later Molly was to confess to me that he had been highly amused by the escapade but had felt it incumbent upon him to crack the whip, *pour encourager les autres*, even though it meant losing a promising manipulator. I put a commendably bold face on it at the time but I was really very upset at being thrown out.

To console myself I opted for extra woodwork instead of puppets on Monday afternoons and was soon turning out ash trays and book-ends by the bushel. For a time even my aero-modelling was pushed into second place. My ancestors on my father's side had been shipwrights and I daresay I inherited something from them. I have always enjoyed using tools and had I been a bit less impatient to see the finished product I daresay I could have scraped some sort of a living for myself as a joiner or cabinet-maker. Unfortunately, because I was good at woodwork—as, indeed, I was at drawing—I discounted both these skills and would willingly have traded them in for an equal talent in Latin and Mathematics. I know now that I was being ridiculous, just as I now know *why* I was, but there, if you are eleven years old and your father is a Classical scholar and a renowned Man of Letters whose approval you desperately want to win, what else can you do?

One afternoon when I was chiselling away industriously in the school workshop the Headmaster strolled in. He wandered around, pipe in mouth, examining the work which was being produced and finally he reached my bench. 'Well, young Jonathan, how's it going?'

'All right, sir, thank you.'

'You've given up the puppets, I hear.'

I flushed. 'Well, yes, sir. Sort of.'

He grinned. 'Too old to be playing with dolls, eh?' He tapped the dottle out of his pipe, blew down the stem and then patted the bowl thoughtfully against his palm. 'How would you like to build a canoe?'

'*A canoe!*'

'That's right. You could do it, couldn't you?'

'I don't—Well, yes, sir . . . I *think* so. But . . .'

'But what?'

'Well, wouldn't it cost an awful lot, sir?'

'Three pounds, fifteen, all in.'

He might just as well have said five hundred pounds. I shook my head. 'Oh, I don't think my father . . .'

'He thinks it's a great idea.'

I gawped. 'You've *asked him*, sir?'

Lee-Browne grinned. 'Well, let's say I happened to mention it in passing.'

'And he's agreed?'

'That's right.'

'Crikey!' I breathed, and already in my mind's eye I was seeing myself and Gordon paddling down the Thret and exploring those mysterious, reed-fringed meres around Wretham.

'Do you think you could have it ready by Founder's Day?'

I nodded dreamily.

'Good. I'm planning a canoe regatta on the lake. The more boats the merrier. It'll give you a target to aim at, won't it? I'll go and have a word with O.G.M.'

I spent the rest of that afternoon in a hazy rapture. By one of those flukes which, from time to time, have convinced me—albeit temporarily—that I have a guardian angel, the Headmaster's proposal had coincided almost exactly with my own discovery of Richard Jefferies' *Bevis*. I had come across a short extract from this minor classic in the prose and poetry anthology which Robin Wilson had issued to us as class readers. Browsing through it during prep one evening, I had stumbled upon the description of Mark's fishing from the raft. At that instant the Big School had simply ceased to exist for me. I was there beside Mark—*was* Mark, rather!—watching the sky-blue float slide and dip beneath the ripples; feeling the stomach-clenching thrill of that first imperious tug at the rod tip which betokens a fish of over a pound; knowing, above all, why, long after the fish had ceased to bite, Mark just went on sitting there while the evening shadows lengthened across the lake and the moorhens clucked and fussed among the shallows. For the first time the life I lived in my imagination and the life I had actually experienced had clasped hands across the printed word. Jefferies came to meet me half way.

No sooner was prep over than I hurried into the library, hunted along the shelves and found two books by him—*Bevis* and *The Story of My Heart*. Within a week I had read *Bevis* twice through from cover to cover and was looking forward to starting on it for a third time. I had also dipped into *The Story of My Heart* but had given it up when I failed to discover anything about fishing. Even so, in the opening chapter I had been able to recognize the record of an experience not unlike some of my own; except that, in my case, I signally lacked Jefferies' marked consciousness of 'self'. I had not yet reached the point where I could say with any real conviction: "I felt myself, myself." In fact it made me feel slightly bewildered just to read the words in print.

Over the years I have come across very few writers who can successfully communicate the mysterious fascination of fishing. Leo Walmsley is, I think, the best of them but, unlikely though it may seem, he is to my mind run a very close second indeed by George Orwell. The chapters in *Coming Up For Air* where 'Fatty' Bowling describes his boyhood passion for angling, capture quite perfectly, both the manner in which a boy can succumb to the spell and, once enthralled, can never wholly escape it again. I did not read *Coming Up For Air* until the war was half over and I can still recall the weird sense of 'double-take' I experienced as I suddenly connected 'George Orwell' with the thin-faced man with a crew-cut who had discussed the merits of different kinds of bait with me on the lawn at The Adelphi Centre one hot afternoon. His suggestion that I tried mixing a drop of oil-of-verbena with my flour and water paste proved so successful when I eventually got round to trying it out that I was moved to write and tell him so. It must have made a change from the sort of letters he was used to getting. In his reply he put me on to Isaac Walton, suggesting, most sensibly, that I tried reading *The Compleat Angler* as a text book. He also lamented the way in which class snobbery had since drawn a line between fly fishing and bait fishing and expressed the hope that I would agree with old Isaac's views on the matter. I'm happy to say that I did and that I still do.

I soon discovered that building a thirteen foot kayak was a very different proposition from constructing book-ends. Luckily there was a wealth of experience for me to draw on since the construction of canoes had been encouraged at Rendcomb for several years and there was already a sizable fleet in existence. In those days there were no power tools available and each inch of boat was bought with a blister. However, my enthusiasm was such that I even arranged to be woken up at six o'clock each morning so that I could get in an hour and a half's carpentry before breakfast. By the end of term most of the basic work had been completed and, when I got back to Larling, I was able to announce proudly to my father that my canoe would be finished by Easter. I thought he seemed surprised.

J.M.M., Betty and Mary, 1937

Col and David, 1940

J.M.M. and Ruby, Walton-on-the-Naze, 1937

Weg

Col

One of the first things I noticed on my return was that Betty was pregnant. Another was that my father looked a lot older. The lines on his face seemed to have deepened and his forehead resembled a lump of cobbler's wax so criss-crossed was it with wrinkles. He moved more slowly too, and, if he had been a clockwork motor I should have felt it was high time to wind him up again. I asked Rue if there had been a lot of rows while I was away and she told me they'd been 'something terrible'.

'How about the prayers?' I enquired.

'Oh, that's all finished. She chucked the prayer book on the fire. Same with the lessons.'

'What lessons?'

'Your dad was helping her with her writing. Didn't you know?'

'No.'

'He's a saint,' mused Rue. 'A real saint. As for her . . .'

'Is it true he's going to be a parson?'

She nodded. 'He's fixed to go to college at Cambridge for a year.'

I considered this glumly. 'You don't suppose he'll want to baptise me, do you?'

Rue cackled. 'You can bet your life I'll be there when he does!'

'Seriously, Rue. Do you think he *will* be a Rev.?'

'How should I know?'

'We'd have to move from here, wouldn't we?'

'I suppose so.'

'Well, let's hope he doesn't,' I said fervently.

25

AT the beginning of January I went to Belgium with Weg for a fortnight's holiday. She was to stay with a school friend of hers called Claire

Truffaut; I was to stay with the Simons. I had previously assumed that I would be together with Weg and, in consequence, had rather been looking forward to the experience; when I discovered this was not the plan I took a distinctly gloomy view of the situation. 'But I don't speak French,' I protested to her. 'I won't be able to talk to anyone.'

'Oh, don't worry about that,' she assured me. 'Irène speaks English.'

'Who's she?'

'Louise's younger sister. You'll like her.'

'Won't Louise be there, then?'

'No. She's in Paris.'

The holiday started badly. During the night crossing from Harwich to Antwerp I was violently seasick into the shoes of a Flemish gentleman who was occupying the bunk below mine. He took it very well, considering, and gave me something colourless to drink out of a flat bottle. I took a huge gulp of what seemed like molten lava and remember nothing more till I woke up and found we were half way up the Schelde estuary.

My recollections of that fortnight are oddly surrealistic. Papa Simon, Louise and Irène's father, was a retired professor. He dressed all in black, had a long white beard, spoke not a word of English and took me for daily '*promenades*' along the slate-grey, cobble-stoned boulevards beside the inky river Meuse. He kept up a running commentary the whole time and, though I understood hardly anything he was saying, I did pick up a few useful words. 'Merde!' he would exclaim, pointing first with his walking stick to a pile of steaming horse-dung and then to the bird-droppings which encrusted the stone parapets of the Meuse bridges like grey icing-sugar. 'Eh voilà! Encore de la merde!'

I began to appreciate both his sense of priorities and the virtues of the direct method. 'Merde?' I piped exultantly, pointing to a dog's turd.

'Oui. Bien sûr!' he applauded. 'C'est un trésor véritable!'

He conducted me around various museums which, for some reason I could not then fathom, all appeared to be called

'Libraries'. Since for the most part they were filled with showcase after showcase of rifles and bayonets, my sense of disorientation was increased still further. Each '*promenade*' ended with him taking me into a café and treating us both to coffee laced with cognac. It was amazing how my French improved under the stimulus. I gathered I was not to tell Madame Simon about this when we got home.

My bedroom was right at the top of the house. It contained a simply enormous brass bed, ornamented with a row of vast rococo knobs at either end. The first night I slept in it I disgraced myself by wetting the sheets. I was overcome with shame and determined it should not happen again. But happen again it did the very next night. If I had been embarrassed the first time, now I was mortified. Desperately I cast about for some way to prevent a further recurrence of the disaster, and finally hit upon an ingenious solution. Routing through the Simon's bathroom cabinet I discovered an empty aspirin bottle. On the third night, as soon as I was in bed, I set about manipulating my penis into the neck of the bottle. It was a tight squeeze but in the end persistence triumphed. Things were a bit cramped inside but this I reasoned was all to the good.

I spent a rather restless night, my sleep broken by my waking up at intervals to feel if my stopper was still in place. When the first thin light of dawn filtered into the room I felt all around me and, to my profound relief, discovered that the bed was bone dry. With a happy sigh I reached down to unplug my stopper and—horror!—it was stuck fast! Somehow my companion and comforter had managed to become '*un peu gonflé*' during the night and in doing so had trapped himself. I tried tugging but that only made matters worse and, besides, hurt like hell. Then I remembered how I had once seen Betty remove her wedding ring by rubbing her finger with soap and screwing the ring off. At least it was worth a try. I scrambled out of bed and, with my bottle bouncing around like a bell-clapper, scuttled down to the bathroom.

The only soap I could find was a bath tablet about the

size of a brick and I was just coming to the hair-raising conclusion that I would have to risk my all by smashing the bottle with the lavatory brush when I thought to try the cabinet again. I spied lurking at the back a bottle labelled 'Huile d'—' something. I pulled out the cork and smelt eucalyptus. I dribbled some pungent drops around the neck of my trap, screwed the bottle round and, slowly, painfully, managed to extract myself. Tenderly I soaped off the eucalyptus and swore that next time I'd let Nature run its course and damn the consequences. As it happened the fright I had given myself seemed to have done the trick on its own accord. At least, to the best of my knowledge, I have never wet the bed since. Even so, I should hesitate to recommend my method as a cure for *enuresis*.

I saw remarkably little of Weg during that fortnight and, when I was invited to attend a children's party at the Truffauts' house, it was to find that she had next to no time to spare for me. She chattered away to her friends like a French sparrow and more or less ignored my existence. When she did deign to acknowledge me it was usually to make some remark about me in French to the other children which sent them off into fits of giggles. I began to feel like an exhibit in a freak show, and when it came to playing a game I did understand—a version of hide-and-seek—I went purposely to a part of the house that I knew perfectly well had been placed out of bounds, and hid myself under a bed. I heard the others calling for me and just lay still and said nothing. Of course I was found eventually and simply pretended that I had not understood the rules. They tapped their foreheads with their fingers and giggled harder than ever.

I am positive that Weg did not mean to be unkind; it was just that she was not really sufficiently sure of herself to be able to put her new-found allegiance to the test. She had won herself a place in a group which accepted her and I, being foreign and different *and* her brother, represented a threat to her fragile security. In a vague, instinctive way I even realized this at the time, but it did not make me feel any happier.

When I got back to the Simons' that night I felt lonelier than I had in years. Furthermore the few phrases of French I *had* acquired seemed to have been driven right out of my head. I mumbled some sort of goodnight to Mama and Papa and trailed away upstairs to bed. A little while later Irène came up. She asked me (in English) what was the matter. She put the question so gently, so sympathetically, that I promptly burst into tears. Whereupon she took me into her arms and comforted me in the only way I could possibly have been comforted. I have long since forgotten what she said, but I do remember that she cried too. At the time it did not strike me as being in any way strange that she should do so.

From the vantage point of hindsight I can see that holiday in Belgium as demarcating some sort of watershed in my childhood. Certainly it alerted me to a subtle change in my relation with my sister. I now sensed that she had altered in a way that I had not fully appreciated before; that somehow she had acquired a passport to a whole continent of experience to which I was a total stranger. But in any case 1938 would have been a significant year in my life. It brought, besides the birth of my step-brother David, the opening skirmish in my father's grim and protracted struggle against Bürger's disease. It was also, I now realize, the year during which I was to discover that thirteen-year-old diary which told me all I was ever to learn about the circumstances surrounding my own birth.

Bürger's disease is a narrowing of the arteries and the veins, especially in the legs, which afflicts heavy smokers. It causes numbness, increasingly severe muscular pain, and may lead to gangrene of the afflicted limb. My father consulted a specialist who advised him to go into a nursing home for a course of diathermy and massage. If this proved unsuccessful it would almost certainly be necessary for him to undergo a major operation within a year.

I received a letter from him when he was in the nursing home. It contained an extremely amusing description of an ingenious method he had worked out for measuring exactly how many circuits of the central flowerbed he would have to complete to cover a mile. I wish I had kept that letter, for the comic facet of his complex character was one I was allowed to glimpse only rarely. But I never forgot it existed. There was a vein of the purest fantasy in him by means of which he was able to recount some quite ordinary event like filling his fountain pen and to transform it into a titanic struggle upon which the fate of empires hung. It was a side of himself which he showed only to those he loved and they, having once seen it, could never wholly understand how others, less privileged, persisted in regarding him as nothing but a remote and desiccated intellectual.

At the end of May, while my father was still in hospital, David was born. When I arrived home for the summer holidays Betty gave me a blow-by-blow account of her labour which I found extremely interesting. I was also intrigued by the apparatus which my father had brought back with him to enable him to continue his treatment. It consisted of a battery of stopwatches, rubber tubes, bladders and pumps for which he had constructed a neat wooden frame to span his bed. I came in to watch him operating his machinery one morning and thought to ask him whether he would have to take the whole contraption with him to Cambridge. He shook his head. 'That's all off, old boy. Didn't I tell you?'

'You mean you're not going to be a parson?'

'Nope.'

'Oh, I *am* glad!' I blurted out. 'I didn't want to be baptized a bit.'

He laughed. 'I'll let you into a secret, old boy. I'm rather relieved too.'

My father was too preoccupied to bother with my Latin lessons that summer and I was left very much to my own devices. Frank Lea, who had taken over most of the day-to-day work on *The Adelphi*, was now lodging in two rooms at the back of the house. Here, as well as coping with his editorial problems, he was struggling to write a book on Shelley. Most days after tea he would accompany me on long rambles across the countryside. He was an ideal walking companion, full of fascinating bits of information about every sort of topic, and he was especially knowledgeable about flint implements of which we discovered several. What I liked particularly about him was that he never talked down to me and listened quite seriously to what I had to say.

Naturally, living under our roof, Frank had first-hand experience of Betty. His methods of dealing with her were somewhat akin to my own and indeed earned him the accolade of 'another bloody giddy goat!' I recall one occasion when we were both helping Ruby to dry up after tea and he had the misfortune to break the lid of Betty's favourite tea pot. This was just the sort of thing to trigger off a monumental explosion and Rue and I were liquid with apprehension. Frank seized the teapot in one hand and the broken lid in the other, rushed upstairs to where Betty was resting on her bed, and flung himself down on his knees before her in an excruciatingly funny parody of grovelling self-abasement. Betty, who was already starting to work herself up into a rage, was moved first to grin and then, after calling him 'a bloody idiot', to laugh out loud. Rue and I grabbed our chance, joined in, and the row was defused.

Almost the only visitor that summer was Uncle Richard. He continued to come down to Larling at weekends to give my father some badly needed moral support. If the weather was fine he and I would pile into Frank's ramshackle Morris 8 tourer and the three of us would drive off into the countryside on a sketching expedition. Frank and Richard made a good pair and no doubt the temporary escape from the tensions in the Old Rectory brought out the best in them both. Certainly I recall those trips as oases of laughter in a desert which was becoming ever more bleak and arid.

Any such hopes as we might have been entertaining that David's arrival would somehow mellow Betty were very soon dispelled. If anything she was worse. My father's resolute refusal to meet her on her own chosen ground of physical violence simply had the effect of goading her into a terrifying hysteria during which she was capable of doing almost anything. At breakfast one morning a row which had been simmering since the early hours suddenly boiled over. She snatched up the baby she was nursing and literally flung him across the table at my father. By some sort of miraculous reflex he succeeded in catching the child while Mary let out a piercing wail of terror and Weg and I sat completely numbed with shock.

How my father contrived to produce any work under such pressures almost defies human understanding, yet he wrote two books—*The Price of Leadership* and *The Defence of Democracy*—as well as numerous magazine articles and his regular reviews for *The Times Literary Supplement.* His stamina was incredible but, as he well knew, he was living on borrowed time, and though his mind might refuse to accept the evidence that was everywhere about him, his body could not. By the end of that year he was forced to acknowledge that the first counter-attack on his diseased leg had failed and that if he were not to lose it altogether he would have to undergo a major operation.

At this period of my life I do not think that I was fully aware of the strain my father was being subjected to, or perhaps it would be truer to say that I *was* aware, but that it seemed to me to differ only in degree from what he had suffered for the previous six years. I realized that my own home life was utterly different from that of my school friends—so different, indeed, that I never made any attempt to describe it to them. When I was not at Larling I could hardly believe in it myself, and when I was there I simply crouched down (not always metaphorically either!), clutched my head in my arms, and hoped that it would break over me.

As much as possible I kept out of the house. Day after day I would get up before dawn and go off fishing, taking my lunch with me. After a brief call back at the Old Rectory for tea I would either go off rambling with Frank or would seek out Gordon. Together he and I would hurry to wherever the corn was being cut and 'run' the rabbits which were left isolated by the binder in the diminishing island of uncut grain in the centre of the field. Another ploy I favoured was to offer to take David for a morning 'walk' in his pram. Together with Mary I would set off down the drive. When we reached the tarred road I would uncover my roller-skates which I had previously concealed beneath David's blankets, strap them on, sit Mary in the pram, and set off skating them for miles along the deserted country roads around Larling. At such times, alone in charge of my small sister and still smaller baby brother, I was perfectly happy and thought neither of the future nor the past.

In being thus able to escape I was infinitely more fortunate than Weg. She was now a day pupil at Thretford Grammar School for Girls and although it was a happier place for her than the Boys' School had been for me, it meant that she was never really free of Larling. Betty's jealous persecution of her was unremitting and, at times, quite sickeningly spiteful. Like myself Weg was very fond of Frank, and Betty lost no opportunity to make Weg's life miserable by teasing her about it. There was nothing good-natured in this; it was done specifically to hurt Weg's feelings and more than once I found her weeping quietly to herself after some particularly vicious thrust.

As if this was not enough she was expected to do all her own washing and cleaning and to help Ruby with the cooking and housework at the weekends. I never heard her complain but there must have been many times when her friends in Belgium seemed a terribly long way away. And yet, though I could sympathize with her, feel *for* her, even, whenever I saw her eyes darken and her cheeks turn pale as Betty rounded on her and lashed her with her tongue, I knew that the tide was drawing us apart inexorably. Both lonely in our own ways we were now drifting off along divergent courses, and hers was even lonelier than mine.

26

MY father underwent his operation in April 1939. It entailed the severing of the nerves which controlled part of the arterial system in his right leg. Unfortunately the surgeon who performed the operation was not primarily a neurologist and although he succeeded in excising the ganglion he damaged something else in the process. The consequence, as my father later recorded, was that: "when, after a month, I emerged from hospital, it was to endure a further six weeks of fantastic pain. . . . The outer world became quite unreal. I walked, or sat, in it as in a transparent cage of pain. No dope—or none that I was given—had the faintest effect upon it. My recollection is that for those six weeks I never slept at all."

What followed is best told in his own words. He wrote the account some eight years later and, as he himself realized, the experience he is describing in it was decisive for his life.

> "Quite suddenly, it ceased. Timidly, incredulously, I entered into life again like a baby fifty years old. And I went off, almost immediately, to a friend's house in Wales where I had been invited to convalesce. I stood on the station platform one mid-May morning and marvelled that the sun shone warm on me, and I was alive: weak, almost imbecile, but indubitably alive. I made the long journey in a quiet ecstasy of painlessness. To prove that I was alive, and that the operation had done its work, I went next morning for a long, but slow and steady walk, of nearly six miles; then in a motor-boat down the river towards Milford Haven; then out to tea with some friends of my friend.
>
> It began in the middle of tea-time. Suddenly, I felt very queer indeed. Not with pain—it had nothing to do with pain. As my consciousness translated the extraordinary and terrible sensation, it was that I was certainly going mad. Since I have been told that people who think they are going mad, never do; while those who do, never think they are (which I can well believe), and, anyhow, I did not go mad, my consciousness was all wrong. What it was doing was to

describe this utterly intolerable sensation in the only terms that seemed appropriate to it. But certainly it seemed to me that I was on the brink of a spiritual abyss, some vast internal void. I tried to behave like a normal person till the unending tea-party was ended. I clutched my chair, to give me confidence, and answered questions as best I could, astonished that the replies were not gibberish. I got away safely into the car. 'I'm feeling queer', I said to my friend. 'Hellishly queer!'

I cannot really remember what happened then, for the next few hours. Somehow, I think, I must have got through dinner and the night. I remember another walk, in the morning, during which, as I walked slowly up the tree-lined road, I knew it was only a question of minutes. I was overwhelmed by the longing to get home, to get into the warm safety of my wife's arms, even while I loathed and despised myself for the longing. But the Terror beside me, within me, waiting for me, was too awful. My fear—or the fear that was me—was such that it would have blotted out all the past. My friend, I knew, would willingly have sent me home posthaste in a fast car across England. But it would be in vain. I should be mad before I got there. The thought and the longing left me.

That night, at dinner, my teeth began to chatter—to my inward ear like castanets. As good fortune would have it, a doctor, who was an old friend of mine, was in temporary practice some twenty-five miles away. I rang him up and tried to explain what had happened. He said I was to come immediately; he would have a bed ready for me. I was there within three-quarters of an hour. Within two minutes he had given me a powerful shot of adrenalin, tucked me up in bed with a big cup of hot tea at my side. Almost instantly the drowsy magic worked. The terror was gone, and a feeling of warm fatigue rose up within me like life itself. I passed the night somewhere between wake and sleep, absolutely happy.

But those six weeks of physical pain, followed by those

three days of unspeakable Fear were the grimmest of my life. Their grimness lay in the fact that they did not belong to life at all. They were outside the range of permissible experience. I have never been able to incorporate them into my own history. The pattern was, for the time being, absolutely broken. But the difference between this rupture, and the rupture of anaesthesia, was absolute, because there was no interruption of consciousness itself. Where 'I' had got to, God alone knows: but the consciousness, of pain, of terror, was there all the while.

It took me another fortnight, mainly in bed, to get rid of my terror completely; and for a few days I was haunted by the fear that it would return. But copious draughts of a black medicine that seemed like the elixir of life to me, and the reassuring explanations of my doctor friend, gradually expelled the Fear. 'You were completely exhausted when you came to Cresselly. You had undergone a major mutilation, from which you had been prevented from recovering by your pain.' At this point he burst into a diatribe, well-deserved, against his professional colleagues who will not make a proper use of drugs. 'You monstrously overtaxed your strength by that fantastic walk, when you should have been in bed, or at most in a deck-chair. No wonder the whole show collapsed. No wonder all the suppressed dread of the last six years of your damnable life came out and engulfed you—in a classical example of the Nervous Breakdown.' "

The doctor, needless to say, was Jimmy Young.

When, at the end of May, my father returned to Larling he was, in effect, a different man. He recognized the nature of the change in himself even though Betty did not, and he described it thus:

"The last tenuous and forlorn wisps of the aura of affection that had once united me to the woman to whom I was married had completely disappeared. I saw her in a hard clear light, with not a trace of warmth or radiance in it.

I felt an immense pity for her, but no love. That had been finally killed. And the reason why I pitied her was that she had killed my love for her. It must have taken an almost superhuman will to do that. I looked at her now as a creature from another place. I said to her quietly, soon after my return, when for some trivial and indeed unreal offence she was storming at me in a violent passion: 'Please take this seriously. I don't love you any more.'

Of course, she did not take it seriously. Had she been capable of doing so, that part of my life which was now ending would have been quite different. But it was true. And it seems clear to me in retrospect that the last tie had been broken when I had resigned myself to the impossibility of fleeing from the Terror into her arms. Then, in the very depths of my psyche (or my psycho-somatic being) the severance was made. . . .

I find it in the last degree illuminating. The condition to which it put an end was a life of spiritual torment which was so exhausting to my bodily energies that the life had begun to withdraw from my body. My six years of spiritual mortification had culminated in the declared and obvious beginnings of physical mortification. The gangrene of my soul had become the gangrene of my body. To check this purely physical mortification I underwent a severe operation, and a subsequent extremity of physical pain, which so weakened my total being that, under the strain of a fresh physical exertion, I sank down into a condition of absolute terror. That terror created its myth: the myth that I was on the brink of a spiritual abyss, which I called 'madness'. Any other name would have done: not-Being, *le néant*, nothingness. And that very nameless Terror held me back from returning to that condition which was the first cause of the Terror itself—that soul-destroying persistence of a physical bond between a man and a woman when the spiritual bond of Love has been worn away. From that the Terror saved me; and its salvation of myself was final. In that strange paroxysm of my psycho-somatic being, the last remnants of the animal bond between the woman and myself were dissolved completely away. The Terror had extirpated its own root."

When I met my father on my return to Larling in July I was taken aback at the physical change in him. I had been given no information on how ill he had been and, naturally, I had no idea of the nature of the spiritual crisis he had undergone. To me he seemed to have shrunk. His hair was several shades greyer and the tendons in his neck and along the backs of his hands stuck out like exposed roots. But there was something else too—a sort of vague, day-dreamy remoteness which puzzled me almost more than his altered appearance. He asked me about Rendcomb and told me that Lee-Browne had suggested it might be a good plan if I gave up Latin and concentrated on art and woodwork instead. I had known this was coming and had been rather worried that he might oppose it, but in fact he simply nodded and observed with a wry smile that, in the circumstances, it seemed a sound notion. Appreciating those circumstances at least as well as he did I agreed wholeheartedly.

A few days later my canoe arrived by rail and was unloaded outside the garage. My father limped down to look at it and was visibly impressed. 'You know, that's a remarkably fine piece of work, old boy. I had no idea it would be such a professional job. Congratulations.'

As casually as I could I directed his attention to the various 'improvements' I had incorporated in the original design. He listened, nodded soberly, and enquired whether there was to be an official launching ceremony. 'But it's already *been* launched,' I pointed out. 'For the school regatta last summer. Don't you remember, I wrote to you about it?'

'Oh, yes,' he said. 'That's right. So you did. I'd forgotten.'

I spent the next few days constructing a trailer and, when it was complete, Frank helped me to wheel the canoe the mile or so down to the river. We launched it in the deep bend behind the church. Apart from a family of suspicious swans we had the river to ourselves. The next day I took Gordon out, and thereafter spent much of my time on the water.

All that summer there was a curious atmosphere of what can best be called 'brooding calm' over the Old Rectory. There were rows, of course, but they seemed to me to lack something of the old frenzy. Perhaps this was in part due to the international crisis but, if so, I am certain it was not a major part. For years my sister and I had known that another world war was inevitable, simply because my father had said so and in such matters we trusted him implicitly. The notion neither depressed me nor excited me. It was just something which would happen. I believed it would start with massive air-raids on the cities, raids in which hundreds of thousands of innocent people would be gassed or blown to bits with high explosive. I had said as much to my friends at school and had been listened to with a certain degree of scepticism. 'Guernica was just the beginning,' I told them darkly. 'You'll see.'

Yet though I prophesied doom I was, *au fond*, no more politically aware than they were. It was just that the scraps of conversation I had picked up from my father and his socialist or pacifist friends were rather different from the average. My father belonged to a generation which had been shattered both literally and metaphorically by the First World War. Like Max Plowman he envisaged the coming conflict as a sort of universal death sentence—the onrush of that 'black wave' which D. H. Lawrence had so clearly foreseen. For a few days after the German invasion of Poland he went down into the uttermost depths of despondency. Then, as week followed week, and the 'Phoney War' dragged out with still no sign of the massive onslaught in the West which he had predicted, his hopes began to revive. What was even more strange was that interest *in him* began to revive too. The B.B.C. approached him and commissioned a series of broadcast talks on the social causes leading up to the war.

In these six short talks, published afterwards under the title of *Europe in Travail*, he reiterated the theme which he had been hammering away at in *The Adelphi* for the past ten years, namely that the root cause of the war was man's failure to master the machine. He concentrated on the single all-important issue of unemployment and stressed and re-stressed the awful paradox of Twentieth Century civilization that "modern society has found no way of keeping its machines running and its members at work, save by preparing for war." He informed the nation at large that the war in which they were engaged was not just a crisis in the fortunes of the British nation but in the history of the whole of mankind.

The impact of these talks was quite extraordinary. The Old Rectory was inundated with fan mail; hundreds and hundreds of letters, some hysterically abusive—even, on occasion, excremental!—some plain cranky, but the vast majority wholly appreciative. He had spoken to ordinary people; tried to explain things as he saw them in a way they could understand; and he had succeeded beyond all expectation. So much so, in fact, that even the Chamberlain government woke up and began to take notice. Sour questions were asked in the House as to why a noted Pacifist and erstwhile Communist should have been allowed the Freedom of the Air when the nation was supposedly engaged in a life-or-death struggle with the sworn enemies of civilization. The point was well made, and although my father protested in a letter to *The Times* that he was not a Communist Party member and never had been, many, many more years were to pass before he was to be invited to broadcast again.

The effect all this notoriety had upon me was to make me realize that having the name 'Middleton Murry' meant that people who previously had never noticed me at all now stopped me and asked me questions I could not answer. One or two even asked me if I could get my father to inscribe copies of books by him which they possessed. Thus it came about that when I travelled home for the Easter Holiday in 1940 I had stowed away in my suitcase sundry volumes of *Keats and Shakespeare*, *Europe in Travail* and *The Evolution of an Intellectual.*

I descended from the train at Harling Road station and looked along the platform for a sign of either Betty or my father. There was no one. I supposed it was possible my telegram had not arrived. Then, as the train pulled away, I saw Bodge waving at me from the gate on the far side of the tracks. I hurried to meet him. 'Hello, Bodge!' I cried. 'Why isn't the car here?'

Bodge looked uncomfortable. 'Ah, well now, m'old dear,' he said. 'That's a bit of a story.'

My heart dropped like a stone down a well. 'Not *more* rows?'

''Fraid so.'

'What about, Bodge?'

He scooped up my suitcase and lodged it across the frame of his bike. 'I daresay you'll be hearing soon enough. Seems like your Dad's got himself into some proper hot water this time.'

'Oh God,' I groaned. 'And I was looking forward to the holidays.'

27

I SOON learnt what lay behind Bodge's words. The atmosphere when I reached the Old Rectory was worse than anything I had ever experienced. A sort of awful pall seemed to hang over the house and though Weg, Mary and Rue seemed glad to see me I rapidly gained the impression that they each had an invisible ear cocked for disaster. As usual it was Rue who enlightened me. Betty had discovered that since the previous summer my father had been 'carrying on' with another woman. She had found one of the letters they were exchanging and since then she had 'gone fair mad'.

Rue was retailing this to me in the kitchen after supper when suddenly we heard Mary cry out: 'Oh Mummy, don't! *Don't!*' A door slammed violently: footsteps pounded along the landing and young David began to howl. I heard Betty's voice raised in a scream of frustration and then the sound of fists pummelling violently on a locked door. 'Come on, Rue,' I groaned. 'Hadn't we better see what we can do?'

To my astonishment she shook her head. 'It's no use,' she said. 'You'd best keep out of it.'

With my stomach wound up like a ball of string I climbed the back stairs. Outside the bathroom door I found Betty, wild-eyed and utterly terrifying, shrieking abuse at the top of her voice. Mary was sobbing bitterly in the doorway to the nursery. Somewhere in the distance I could hear Weg trying to soothe young David. I drew in a deep breath, laid my hand on Betty's arm and coaxed her gradually away from the locked door. 'Come on, Ma,' I said. 'What good will that do?'

Incredibly, she allowed me to lead her back along the landing. All the time she was raving on about 'that fucking drunken whore'. Her face was wet with tears. I guided her into her bedroom and, after a minute or two, she calmed down a bit and even began to appeal to me. 'I've been a good wife to him, haven't I?' she grizzled. 'You know I have. I've cooked for him, I've slaved for him, I've kept this house lovely and brought up you kids and now look what he goes and does to me! I nursed him through his operation. He would have died without me. He's filth, that's all he is, Col. Filth!' On and on she went, rambling from one non-sequitur to another while I patted her arm and assured her that she was a good mother to us all and that my father was a wicked, perverted monster. Quite frankly at that moment I would have agreed with anything. When I eventually managed to escape back downstairs I found I was trembling inwardly so much that it was all I could do to prevent myself from being physically sick.

The pattern thus established remained virtually unchanged for the rest of the holiday. When a row was not actually in progress Betty was brooding darkly over her injuries. Mary and young David seemed to spend much of the time in tears. The irony of it was that in spite of her constantly reiterated refrain of what a good wife she had been and how she was his 'unpaid housekeeper' and 'slaved her fingers to the bone' Betty was, by nature and inclination, extremely idle. Her favourite occupation was to lie on her bed and sulk. Had it not been for Ruby and Weg the household would long since have degenerated into hopeless chaos. When Betty did stir herself she was usually in such a vile temper that everyone exhausted themselves in the effort to humour her. The psychic tension she contrived to generate was unbelievable. The whole household was united in the single aim of propitiating her. We might as well have been building sandcastles to hold back the tide. By the end of that summer holiday it was quite clear to me that as long as my father and she were living under the same roof, life in any normally accepted sense of the word would be absolutely impossible.

How my father could not realize this also is something I have never understood. He persisted in believing that somehow a miracle would happen and Betty would change her nature. Yet it was precisely his own black and bitter despair ouer the possibility of this ever happening that had driven him to seek someone who could return his love. Having found her, his own belief in love was restored and he discovered within himself the strength to go on. What he did not see—or did not seem to see—was that in doing so, far from making life easier for his children, he was making it well-nigh unbearable. Betty was not just *his* cross, she was ours too and, unlike himself, we had no external love source to draw upon for sustenance.

Admittedly we had each other, but the strain of conflict to which we were increasingly subjected often seemed to make this loyalty more apparent than real. Betty was tireless in driving the wedge between us. Mary and David were *her* children; Weg and I were *his*. 'You take your two children,' she would whine, 'an' I'll take mine. An' I'll keep Larlin', darlin'.' I would look across at Mary and see her eyes huge and dark with the shadow of unshed tears. David would turn bewildered from one to another and his face would pucker up preparatory to a wail of dismay. And I would feel sick all over again.

At night I would lie awake and listen to Betty's voice droning on and on in a flat and deadly monotone. I would fall asleep at last with its poison dripping in my ear and awake in the morning to hear it still there. It etched itself so indelibly upon my memory that sometimes it seems to me that I can still hear it even though Betty herself has now been dead for over twenty years.

The sole avenue of escape remaining to me was Gordon, Frank Lea having left at the outbreak of the war and gone to join Max Plowman at Langham. Gordon was now doing piece-work for a big canning company that farmed a thousand acres around East Harling. In May he had joined the newly formed Home Guard and by the time I got back in the summer he had already established a reputation for himself as an outstanding marksman. He mentioned shyly to me that he had been ear-marked as a sniper. We discussed the war together and I told him I was going to try to get into the Fleet Air Arm.

'What does your Dad think of that?' he asked.

'I haven't told him yet,' I said. 'But I don't suppose he'll mind. Anyway it's years ahead yet.'

On the last evening of that summer holiday Gordon and I decided to go fishing. I collected him shortly after six and we biked off to our favourite pitch behind the church. We fished for a couple of hours and neither of us had a single bite to boast of. Finally in exasperation Gordon squeezed up all the rest of his bait into a lump the size of a crab apple, stuck it on his hook and slung it out into the middle of the stream. Then we each lit up one of his Woodbines and wandered off along the river bank.

We returned to our rods half an hour later. 'Bugger the bloody fishing!' grumbled Gordon and heaved his out of the reeds where he had left it. Whereupon, to his utter amazement, his whole rod bent like a bulrush in a gale and the line, taut as a fiddlestring, began to move slowly off across the surface of the water. 'Christ all bloody mighty!' he gasped. 'What is it, Karl?'

His face was such a study of astonishment that I exploded into wild laughter. Gordon heaved and heaved. Finally a vast, fan-shaped dorsal fin broke the surface, and a mouth the size of a tea-cup was gaping up at us. 'It's a carp!' I howled. 'An enormous bloody great carp!'

The monstrous creature turned over lazily on to its parasite-encrusted side, took a good look at us, sneered, and *ping!* the line snapped. Gordon staggered backwards, tripped, and subsided into an elderberry bush. I laughed so much that I collapsed into a bed of nettles. And Gordon's float moved off serenely, drawing a little arrowing ripple behind it, until it vanished somewhere among the reeds downstream.

28

MY father's literary fortunes which had seemed to be once more upon the ascendant with the *Europe in Travail* broadcasts slipped back into almost complete extinction when France fell in June 1940. A squad of detectives descended upon the Old Rectory and bore away any writings which in their opinion could be connected, however remotely, with those whom Winston Churchill would soon be calling 'the Nar-zees'. Articles which mentioned Nietzsche, Goethe and Reinhold Niebuhr were prominent among the victims. Overnight, it seemed, my father's chief source of income had dried up. *The Times Literary Supplement* turned to other less controversial critics for its middle page articles, while the sequel to *Europe in Travail* which he had called *The Betrayal of Christ by the Churches* and from which he had been hoping for much, appeared in the bookshops just as the London Blitz was at its height and its message was quite drowned out by the explosions. Then, just when it was beginning to look as if he might have to struggle through the war as a professional bee-keeper, the governors of *Peace News*—the official organ of the P.P.U.—offered him the job of editor at a salary of £7 (plus fares) for a three day week. He was glad to take it not just for the meagre income it would provide but because it offered a platform, however modest, for his own views and, at least equally important, the opportunity of regular meetings with the woman who was eventually to become his fourth wife.

He threw himself into his new job with an energy which would have been remarkable in any man, let alone one who was as life-battered as he was. Within eight months, largely by his own effort and inspiration, the circulation of that 'filthy conchie rag', as Betty insisted on calling it, had risen from 9,000 to 18,000 and his own weekly *Commentary*, written under the pseudonym 'Observer', was being perused in quarters which could hardly have been sympathetic to the paper's avowed aims.

Nevertheless, though my father's weekly comments were chiefly concerned with the progress of the war, his editorial policy was ultimately to prepare people for the society which would eventually emerge from its ashes. He was haunted both by the spectre of Versailles and by those faceless millions of whom D. H. Lawrence had written:

But oh, the streams that stream white-faced, in and out
in and out when the hooter hoots, white-faced, with a
dreadful gush
of multitudinous ignominy,
what shall we think of these?

"What this country desperately needs," my father insisted, "is something to believe in. The destruction of Hitlerism is not enough; the Atlantic Charter is not enough; Mr. Churchill is not enough; survival is not enough; and Christianity, in the form in which it now presents itself to the common man, is certainly not enough. What is needed is an image of their own country that can inspire men with a vision of the good life that can be won by their own efforts and their own will. Somehow they have to be convinced, even at the cost of experiencing alarm and despondency, that the Christian values, which are at present still diffused in the British tradition and the British ways of life, are in peril, not so much from Hitlerism as from our own spiritual sloth and mental inertia . . ."

In *Christocracy*, the book he completed in 1941, he put forward his own solution. It was one which, in these days of economic and ecological crisis, seems wholly prophetic. Basically his answer was "a steady effort towards decentralization", a breaking up of the urban-based economy into small integrated units in which each man and woman was to be given individual status. To those who, he foresaw, would criticize this on economic grounds he replied:

"It will be said that such a distribution of industrial enterprise comes into conflict with fundamental economic necessities. Coal mines must be on coal seams; ironworks near iron ore, or in places to which it can conveniently be shipped. We do not deny it. Some basic industries are immovable. But, in the first place, these basic industries are nothing like so important to the national economy as they used to be, except in the incurably vicious conditions of war; and in the second place, their immobility need not prevent us from drastically redistributing those which are mobile. Further, it will be said that by decentralization we lose all the benefits of rationalization—of mass-production and the conveyor-belt. If we want cheap motor cars we can have them only from factories that employ ten or twenty thousand men. I am not so certain that we do need cheap motor cars as badly as all that: I sometimes think they have become a necessity because men are so eager to get quickly away from the kind of places in which they live. But there is no difficulty about drastically decentralizing the manufacture of the innumerable components of your standardized car. Some of it is decentralized already. Decentralize it to the maximum, remembering that your real concern is not the production of the cheapest motor car possible, but the cheapest compatible with a regeneration of the social life of the country.

"It is this sense of the supremacy of the social end that is so hard to get into men's heads. 'Man's life consisteth not in the abundance of goods he possesseth.' Not that abundance of goods is not a good. It is. But it is a good which must, in any sound or Christian social philosophy, be reckoned entirely subordinate to the quality of life men live . . ."

Like so many of his books *Christocracy* was away ahead of its time, the relevance of its message is far more obvious today than it was in 1941. Written during 'Europe's darkest hours', it twinkles like a distant lighthouse, offering a harbour of hope, and is lit from within by that strangely disinterested 'love for mankind' which permeates the work of the early Romantics. That such a book should have been written at such a time and in domestic circumstances of such grinding bitterness, strikes me today as falling but little short of the miraculous.

29

I DARESAY that the emotional turmoil of Larling was in part to blame for the fact that I became something of a Rendcomb 'case' at about this time. This did not signify very much more than that someone in our form had been heard to observe publicly that 'half Form 4 is Form 4 and the other half is the psychological cases'. My academic work plumbed bathyscopic depths and had it not been for an altruistic classmate who set himself the task of patiently re-teaching me the lessons I had been too abstracted to learn in school I should probably have sunk into complete educational oblivion. Even so it began to look as though the odds against my gaining my 'Matric' were lengthening to the point where they verged upon the astronomical. Furthermore I was dogged by bad luck. Wholly by accident I broke a large window and so saddled myself with a sort of private version of the National Debt whereby my small weekly allowance was taxed by about a third; I borrowed someone's fountain pen and promptly lost it; I began to be late for everything; got hauled up before The Council for unsocial behaviour and thereafter spent most of my free afternoons sawing up logs in the stable courtyard as a punishment. I began to feel that everyone's hand was raised against me. It was at this truly dark and dismal point that Sammy Morris entered my life.

Sammy was in the Upper 6th reading for a History scholarship. He was about three years older than I was. His closest friend, a brilliant Austrian Jew by name 'Freddie' Fischer, had been summarily dragged away under the notorious '18B' regulations and was now incarcerated in the Isle of Man preparatory to being despatched to an internment camp in Canada. At the time it did not occur to me that this unhappy event might have had some bearing on the fact that Sammy turned to me for company. At first I was just plain baffled. With part of me I kept wanting to glance over my shoulder to see whether he was not in fact addressing himself to someone else. When he did finally succeed in convincing me that I had been found worthy of his attention I promptly fell in love with him out of sheer gratitude. Someone had actually singled *me* out above all others! *Me!* It was the biggest miracle since the Marriage Feast at Canaan!

For those—if, indeed, there are any such left!—who turn pale at the mere thought of homosexual relationships, it might be as well to point out that what Sammy and I felt for one another was wholly Platonic. This is not to suggest there was no physical homosexuality at Rendcomb—there was—plenty of it—but, to the best of my knowledge, it was confined fairly strictly within the narrow band of one's own age group, just as it had been at Thretford. Maybe there were exceptions to this but, if so, I was not aware of them. Naturally I was subjected to a fair amount of teasing by my class-mates and had to put up with the odd jibe that I was 'Sammy's bum boy', but it was easy enough to shrug these off and, within a month or two, they had stopped altogether.

What then *did* our relation amount to? Looking back I find it extraordinarily difficult to decide. Fundamentally, I think, we enjoyed being in each other's company. We went for long aimless walks together; we laughed a lot; and we talked endlessly. One day when we were strolling in the park Sammy produced a couple of sheets of paper and handed them to me. They contained the draft of a longish poem in blank verse which he had composed. I read it through and tried to make head and tail of it, but without much success. Finally I handed the sheets back, telling him I'd think about it and would give him my opinion when I'd decided what it was.

Sammy grinned. 'It's that bad, is it?'

'No, no,' I protested. 'It's just that I can't be sure *what* I feel about it.'

'Then it's no good,' he said. 'If you'd said you weren't sure what you *thought* about it I'd have let it go. But I trust your *feelings* one hundred percent.'

I looked at him in surprise. Such a simple thing and I had never considered it before. 'You're right,' I said wonderingly. 'It was just that I didn't want to upset you by saying I didn't like it.'

He nodded, handed me back the poem and said: 'O.K. So now tell me what you don't like about it. And for Christ's sake trust your instinct.'

I sat down on the grass, re-read the poem from beginning to end and suddenly realized that I knew perfectly well what was wrong with it. It lacked imaginative intensity. Reading it was like peering down into cloudy water: the images were blurred and diffuse where they should have been distinct. I told him so.

Sammy argued ably and hard in his poem's defence, but he was on the retreat all the time and, oddly enough, he seemed to relish my newfound confidence in my own opinions. 'If only you'd *believe* in yourself a bit more,' he chuckled, 'you'd have old Robin eating out of your hand in next to no time.'

For me that conversation had the impact of a genuine spiritual revelation. To be able to believe in myself, all I needed was someone else who would believe in me too. And here was Sammy doing just that. It was as though I had been swimming desperately for my life in three feet of water. I put my foot down and found I was standing on rock. I drew in my breath and looked about me.

What I perceived straight away was that the barrier which had always interposed itself between what I was able to visualize so clearly and what I was able to describe in words was, in fact, no barrier at all. It had simply ceased to exist. I stepped straight through into the world of my own imagination and, like a reporter, set about recording what I found there.

Since I certainly had no burning message I wished to impart, I wrote for the most part short stories and sketches in which I featured only as an invisible but all-seeing eye. I peeped through imaginary key-holes. What I saw was usually miserable and occasionally grotesque. Norman Stone read some of my sketches and pronounced them 'not at all bad'. Then one day Robin Wilson asked me if he could see what I was working on. I handed over my two exercise books, thinking to hear nothing more for at least a fortnight, but that very same evening I was brought a message by a breathless junior that Mr Wilson would like to see me up in his room.

I found Robin pouring a bottle of sherry into a cut-glass decanter. 'Come along in, John!' he cried cheerily. 'This is terrible stuff to be sure, but I daresay I can persuade you to join me in a glass.'

He recorked the empty bottle and decanted two substantial tots, one of which he handed to me. 'Here's long life and happiness to us all,' he murmured.

'Your good health, sir,' I responded and took a hearty swig. It was Irish whiskey!

'Well now,' he said, gesturing me into an armchair, 'wouldn't it just be your damnable luck to have discovered your talent at the very moment when paper rationing prevents me from publishing you in the magazine? After I've put in all that dreary stuff which no one in his right senses ever reads, I've barely room left to swing a sonnet. And your shortest piece is over a thousand words. Ah, if it was only a couple of years ago now I'd have had it in like a shot.'

I blinked across at him tipsily. 'You mean you *like* them sir?'

'I do indeed,' he said. 'They all need polishing, of course—you're far too fond of the adjectives and, frankly, your punctuation's a disgrace—but it's the real thing all right. Sure, but you must know that.'

His words descended upon me like manna. I took another gulp at my drink and tried to concentrate on what he was saying. Something about James Joyce and Frank O'Connor and Chekhov. Since I'd read none of them it didn't mean very much to me but I kept nodding my head and tried to look intelligent.

I left him half an hour later. Under my arm I was clasping three books: a copy of James Joyce's *Dubliners*; one of the little green volumes of the Constance Garnett translation of Chekhov's short stories; and Turgenev's *A Sportsman's Notebook*. My education proper had at last begun.

A few weeks later Sammy went up to Oxford to sit for his scholarship. He was away for three days; quite long enough for me to appreciate how deeply attached to him I had become and to experience an unpleasant foretaste of what Rendcomb would be like without him. During his absence I occupied myself at the lathe in the workshop turning a bowl in black-walnut which I intended as my Christmas present for Betty.

When Sammy returned he was carefully non-committal about his chances, but this I assumed was insurance against failure. In fact he was offered not one Open Scholarship but two! The news of the second arrived on the very last morning of term. The bus which was to take me into Cirencester station had just arrived when Sammy was handed a telegram. I have an eidetic vision of him opening the buff-coloured envelope and then launching into a sort of wild war-dance of triumph as he disappeared, whooping, up the back drive in the direction of J. C. James' house.

A day or two later he wrote to me at Larling apologizing for having abandoned me so unceremoniously. He told me he had applied for a six months' 'pre-war-service' course at Wadham College prior to his going to an O.C.T.U. in a year's time. His place would still be there for him after the war—'if

I'm there to fill it'. I had read this phrase through twice before I realized its full implication. When I did finally grasp it it brought the reality of war home to me as nothing else had yet been able to.

In the excitement attendant upon Sammy's scholarships I somehow forgot to pack my wooden bowl. I now realized with considerable dismay that not only had I no Christmas present for Betty but I also had no money left with which to buy one. If I had simply gone to her and confessed what had happened it is possible—though by no means probable—that she would have forgiven me. However, at the critical moment my built-in death-wish overcame me. I scribbled a brief note explaining what had happened, wrapped it round an apple, and then proceeded to make up an elaborate 'parcel within a parcel' consisting of layer upon layer of brown paper, cardboard and string. It took me at least an hour to complete but in the end I had produced something that looked truly impressive. Weg and Mary who had watched me at work on it were goggle-eyed with excitement and apprehension. A practical joke on Betty was tantamount to lighting the blue touch paper and then stuffing the firework down your own shirt.

We opened our presents at breakfast time on Christmas morning. Betty's face, which had looked as sour as though she'd spent Christmas Eve sucking lemons, brightened as she caught sight of my handsome and substantial gift. Weg, Mary and I poked each other under the table and Weg gave a nervous giggle. Betty removed the outer layer and discovered another fully-fledged parcel inside. She smiled, called me a bloody fool, and set to work on the string. When this wrapping was removed to reveal yet a third parcel and then a fourth, her smile became distinctly wintry and I began to be aware of the first cold prickles of doubt. Mary and Weg were simply gazing spellbound as the pile of paper and cardboard began to mount ever higher.

My father, who had taken little interest in the proceedings up to this point, now cocked a quizzical eyebrow in my direction. I grinned bravely. Apart from the crackle of wrappings, an ominous hush had fallen over the room. Betty, with her features set like Plaster of Paris, tore her way ever more ferociously towards the kernel of her gift. Long before she got there I realized I was guilty of a grievous error of judgement. Nothing short of the Cullinan diamond would have satisfied her now. In fact when she eventually reached my note she didn't even bother to read it: she simply hurled the apple at me, kicked over her chair, and lunged for me. I dodged round the table yelping that I was sorry, that it was all a mistake. Then, realizing I hadn't a hope in hell, I fled upstairs and hid. I heard her yelling for my blood and my heart fainted within me.

Most of Betty's rages against me were fairly short-lived. This one lasted for four days and four nights and by the end of it I was a nervous wreck. She subjected me to a campaign of such cold, relentless hatred as I could scarcely have believed possible even from her. Finally, in despair, I stole five shillings which Aunt Doll had sent to David as a birthday present, cycled off into East Harling with it and bought a little china bowl as a peace offering.

For a moment after I had handed it to her I thought my stratagem had worked. She seemed, grudgingly, to be on the point of forgiving me. Then her lips thinned and her nose sharpened. 'Where did you get the money?'

'I—I had it.'

'You're lying. You stole it, didn't you?'

'No. No I didn't.'

She walked straight over to the bureau where the money had been, pulled out the little drawer and extracted the now empty envelope. 'You're a liar and a thief too. Just you wait till your father hears about this.' As she said this, she smiled. That smile was terrifying.

I flung myself upon her. 'Don't tell him,' I begged. 'Please don't tell him.'

'I was right about you, Col,' she said. 'You're just like Weg. Rotten. Rotten right through. You'll both end up behind bars.'

'But you won't tell him, will you? Promise you won't tell him.'

Amazingly she agreed and I crept away once more.

Of course, as soon as my father returned from London she did tell him. It was what she had intended to do all along. My iniquity was simply another weapon she could use in her endless war of attrition. That evening I crawled into my father's study and made a clean breast of everything to him. He listened to me sadly and then took me in his arms and comforted me. 'It's not really your fault, old boy,' he said. 'We both know that. She's mad—quite mad.'

'But why *does* she hate you so?' I asked.

'I don't know,' he said. 'I really don't know.'

30

THE boost to my self-confidence that Sammy had given me did more than anything to help me face Rendcomb without him. We corresponded regularly and I told him exactly what I was up to. All sorts of moribund interests suddenly revived. I found myself back in the Puppeteers as well as being involved in various stage performances either as an actor or a stage hand. I became secretary to the Aero-Modelling Club; was elected to a couple of minor offices in The General Meeting; and was appointed one of the 'poultry-men' whose job it was to look after the flock of hens the College had recently acquired. Most surprising of all I re-discovered my lost gift for rapid memorizing. The result was that one or two members of staff began to hint that my 'Matric' might not, after all, be such a lost cause as they had supposed. Robin Wilson even went out of his way to let me know that he was counting on having me in his Lower 6th in September. The school report I received at the end of that term was probably the best I had had for five years.

I arrived back at Larling to find things much as they had

been when I had left, the one significant difference being that we had now acquired some lodgers. An Irish Sergeant Pilot and his young wife were occupying the two rooms which had once been Frank Lea's *Adelphi* editorial office. 'Paddy' was stationed at the huge R.A.F. base which had been constructed near Wretham and from which the squadrons of Wellington bombers rose in the twilight to drone off on missions over Germany and Occupied Europe. He had a wry sense of humour. I once asked him what it was like being a bomber pilot and he replied with a grin: 'Ah, you can have no idea what a relief it is to get away from your civil war.'

He spoke with reason. Ruby told me that a fortnight after he had arrived he had rushed down to the garage, locked it and hidden the key, because Betty in one of her crazy fits was threatening to drag young Mary and David into the car and gas them. Each time my father returned from London it was the signal for a fresh outburst of frenzy. When he was away she turned her attention on Weg. Jealousy gnawed at her insides like vitriol. Anything or anyone my father loved was to be attacked and destroyed even though it meant destroying herself in the process. She was possessed by the demon of annihilation and it seemed simply a question of time before his will was done.

Yet, strange as it may seem, her insanity—for in truth I believe it was no less—now had the effect of drawing us four children even closer together. All Betty's attempts to force us apart had proved unavailing. Like grains of quicksilver, no sooner was her malignant attention diverted from us than we coalesced once more and consoled and comforted each other. David, now an angelic, utterly adorable little boy of three, hopelessly bewildered by his mother's extraordinary alternations of mood, stomped around after us and absorbed from us some of the love that was denied him elsewhere.

But we were all, in our different ways, old beyond our years in experience, and we were now deeply suspicious of all outsiders however sympathetic. We might well have taken for our motto Henry IV's retort to his erstwhile comrade-in-arms:

'Go hang yourself, brave Crillon; we fought at Arques and you were not there!' Our perspectives were different from other people's and so too, no doubt, were our values. By a psychiatric reckoning we should all four have been ruined for life but, in fact, only one of us was and he remembered nothing of his first four years. Ultimately it was my father who was responsible for our survival. In spite of everything we each knew not only that he loved us, but that he was laying down his life for us. At that utterly fundamental level we trusted him absolutely, but we knew too that without him alive we were lost. At different times both Weg and I pleaded with him to stay away from Larling, but he was either not convinced that it would be better for us if he did or—and this seems more likely—he was not yet sufficiently certain that his new love would stand the strain which such a severance would bring to bear upon it.

During that Easter holiday I diverted myself by doing a series of ink and water-colour sketches of the landscape around Larling as well as a portrait of Gordon. I showed these to Mr Molineaux when I got back to school. He propped them up, one by one, against an easel in the Art Room and studied each in silence. Finally he nodded. 'You'll do, John.' It was the first time he had ever called me anything except 'Murry'.

From then on the Art Room became my second home and the workshop saw me no more. I flung myself into mastering the techniques of drawing and painting with a single-mindedness that boded ill for my 'Matric'. Molly, I'm happy to say, aided and abetted me in every way, and we agreed between us that I should opt to take Art as one of my Higher Level subjects along with English and History. But before I could do this I had to clear the hurdle of the School Certificate and the closer I got to it the higher it grew. Three weeks before I was due to sit my first paper I set myself to memorize as much as I possibly could in the time available to me. Unfortunately, the one subject where memorizing was of little help was in Mathematics, and, such was the nature of the old School Cert. that unless you passed in Maths you failed your 'Matric'. It still seems as unfair to me today as it did then.

Just before term ended I volunteered in my capacity as poultry-man to stay on at school for the first week of the holidays to look after the chickens. This was by no means as altruistic as it may sound for I had previously arranged with Sammy that he should visit Rendcomb for three days on his way down from Oxford. He was to be accommodated in that same College Guest Room to which, many years before, I had been transferred from the Sick Bay.

At tea time on the day appointed he had still not appeared so, after attending to the hens, I went up to the Guest Room to wait for him. I now found his suitcase lying open on one of the beds, but there was no sign of its owner. On the point of setting off to look for him I caught sight of a bundle of my own letters tucked into a corner of the case. Curious as ever I took one out of its envelope and had just started to re-read it when I heard footsteps in the passage outside. I thrust the letter back and skipped out of the open window, intending to do what I had done many times before, namely step across from one broad window-still to the adjacent one and then climb back in through the open window of the first floor changing room. I stretched across the intervening gap and suddenly, astonishingly, I had lost my balance and was falling.

It seemed an agonizingly slow process. The huge, square, metal, rainwater duct drifted tantalizingly beyond the reach of my clutching fingers: the golden-yellow stone face of the building tilted gently backwards: the sunlit ground-floor windows flicked past: and then I was lying on the gravel path some thirty feet below my launching point, half-stunned, with all the breath knocked out of me.

I scrambled dizzily to my feet and staggered off towards the nearby gymnasium feeling like nothing on earth. My right arm which had been trapped between my body and the brick rim of a drain was hurting abominably, but my sole concern was to get inside the building without attracting anyone's attention. I dared not even glance up to see if Sammy was looking out of the Guest Room window.

I made it somehow and, once inside, sank down on to a pile of gym mats, closed my eyes and waited for the waves of nausea to subside. When they did I looked down at my aching forearm and realized at once that something was seriously the matter with it. It was bent in quite the wrong place and a bump like a fingertip was poking up under the skin just below the new bend. I drew in a painful breath, got to my feet and set off in search of Matron.

She was anything but delighted to see me. 'Well, and what's the matter with you?' she demanded, and before I could tell her she had caught hold of me by the dangling right wrist and lifted my hand. My forearm sagged in the middle and I passed out cold.

That was the end of my carefully laid scheme for getting three days' holiday with Sammy. I was whistled off to the hospital in Cirencester, X-rayed and plaster-casted, and the very next morning was on my way back to Norfolk.

But the malignant Fates had not yet done with me. Betty came down to the station to meet me from the train. As we drove back to the Old Rectory she glanced at me out of the corner of her eye and said: 'I've got some bad news for you, I'm afraid. Gordon's dead.' Just like that.

At first I simply didn't believe her—I *couldn't* believe her. But it was true. He had been knocked over by a lorry, ten days before, and after lying in a coma for thirty-six hours at the hospital, had died without ever recovering consciousness.

It is not easy to convey what Gordon's death meant to me. He had belonged essentially to that 'other Larling'—the happy, sunny one which had always existed apart from the battle-ground of the Old Rectory. When I was away at school and thought about home, as I quite often did, it was that golden countryside I recalled not the house of rows and pain and endless tears. Gordon and I had grown up together, shared so much, and now I would never again hear him say with that soft, intimate Norfolk drawl of his: 'Wotcher, boy Karl. How's she comin' along then?' In my memory I could still crunch beside him across the frozen fens to the reed-cutter's ruined cottage, or stalk the hedgerows for sparrows, or drift with him in the canoe among the lacquered lily-pads. But that was all that was left: memories which slipped through the mind like so much water.

Something in the primitive, almost *animal* quality of my misery touched even Betty and she did her best to jolly me out of it, but I was too numb to respond. At my father's suggestion I went down to see Gordon's mother but, fond as she had been of him, he was but one child among so many and she was plainly perplexed by the intensity of my grief. As I recall it, my visit ended with her doing her best to console *me*! It occurs to me now that, by his death, Gordon somehow broke down the invisible barrier that separated my spiritual home from my real one and allowed the bitterness from one to flood over into the other.

It was weeks before I could bring myself to visit the places which he and I had made our own. Then, one morning early in September, Bodge called me out into the back yard and handed me a rusty tin. 'Reckon you could use those?' he asked.

I peered into the tin. Lying on a scrap of moss at the bottom was a tangle of the little striped worms known as 'brandlings'. There is no more taking bait for perch. 'Where did you get them, Bodge?'

'Over Hockham way. I thought it was about time you did a bit of fishing. Now the arm's mended, I mean.'

'Yes,' I said, and felt a faint vestigial stirring of the old excitement.

Bodge thrust back his cap and scratched his thinning hair. His eyes twinkled. 'I should try up along the Angel bridge, if I 'us you. I saw some big uns there th'other evening.'

'Really?'

He nodded. ''Bout to there, I'd say.' With a forefinger as thick as a well grown carrot he measured off a mark on his jacket cuff.

'You're sure they were perch?'

'Else I'm a Dutchman.' He settled his cap square again and

chuckled. 'Your Dad's very partial to a nice fried perch, I b'lieve.'

After tea I assembled my tackle, got out my bike and cycled off. I had fully intended to try my luck under the bridge as Bodge had suggested but when I was half way down the drive I changed my mind and headed towards the church instead.

I left my bike in the hedge and set off along the track which I had not walked since that evening the previous summer when Gordon had hooked his monstrous carp. The air was dead still, not a leaf moved, and clouds of midges were dancing in the pools of mellow sunlight among the trees. I heard the faint clucking of a moorhen and, as though in answer, an invisible woodpigeon began to coo drowsily in the high elms behind the church tower.

I edged cautiously across a reed-fringed, single-plank footbridge and then ducked my way in and out among the elder clumps and bramble thickets till I reached the river. I had it all to myself. A quarter of a mile upstream half a dozen brown and white cows were standing in the shallows tossing their heads and swishing their tails at the flies. The September sunlight was spread like golden butter across the water-meadows. I gazed about me, drew a deep breath, and had just started to assemble my tackle when I became aware that I was no longer alone. I glanced over my shoulder, fully expecting to see another fisherman wandering along the bank. There was no one. And yet the conviction was so strong that finally I laid my rod down on the grass and called sharply: 'Who's there?'

'*You. You-oo-oo; you-oo,*' crooned the woodpigeon. '*You-oo-oo; you-oo.*'

I shivered violently and felt the hairs along my arms stir as my skin gathered itself up into gooseflesh. A blue dragonfly rattled briskly across the silver surface of the water and settled on the rim of a lily pad. So still was the river that I might have been staring at an enamelled jewel poised above a looking glass. By now my senses were so keyed-up that when a woodpecker began hammering out its rapid *tock-tock-tock* on a dead tree in the woods further downstream it seemed as though it was doing it right beside my ear.

I was not *afraid* exactly, and I certainly did not feel threatened in any way; I was simply—and inexplicably—convinced that I was not alone. Yet I was by no means sure what made me so certain. It was just an absolute *awareness*, no more, no less; and, as I gradually allowed myself to accept it, I discovered that some sentient part of me which had been frozen solid ever since I had learnt of Gordon's death had begun to thaw out. I remember drawing in a breath so deep that my lungs seemed to reach right down into my toes. And then, feeling happier than I had for a month, I began to fish.

Thirty-two years have passed since that experience and yet it seems every bit as real to me now when I recall it as it was then. What does surprise me is that for the first sixteen of those thirty-two years I did my best to discount it. Not until my father died in 1957 and I underwent a second similar experience was I able to accept the first for what it was. In both cases what I had received was an overwhelming assurance that I was not alone. Many people will, I am sure, maintain that I was deluding myself. I cannot help that. To deny the subjective truth of those two events would, as far as I am concerned, be tantamount to a denial of my own human existence.

Although I cannot pretend that I was aware of it in those precise terms, I do not think it would be an unpardonable exaggeration to say that my childhood ended with Gordon's death. After it nothing seemed quite the same any more. It altered my viewpoint on life. When I heard that I had failed my 'Matric' I was depressed, certainly, but nothing like so profoundly as I would have been had the news reached me eight weeks earlier. But the event which really convinced me that I had changed 'in myself' was the final row that exploded on the day before I was due to return to school.

Some time previously my father had made himself a new workshop in the back part of the house. I was in there putting the finishing touches to a marionette I was constructing when I heard the most appalling screams coming from the direction of the front hall. I laid down my file and listened. The screaming came again and there was a sound of muffled blows. I hurried through the dining-room and out into the hall beyond. I found my father half-crouched, half-kneeling in the hallway trying to shield his bowed head from the blows which Betty was raining down on him. She was wholly demented; kicking him; striking at him with her clubbed fists and shrieking abuse at the top of her voice. She seemed to me like some utterly evil bird of prey. I was certain she was about to kill him.

A sort of rage of horror swept over me. I leapt at her, seized her by one upraised arm and dragged her backwards with all my might. I caught her off balance. She staggered back, tripped, and fell heavily. 'Leave him alone!' I screamed. 'Let him be! D'you hear?' I grabbed hold of her arm again, dragged her backwards all along the floor to the drawing-room, then ran back to my father.

His face was like grey, scribbled parchment and he blinked up at me like someone groping his way fearfully up out of the burrow of some horrible nightmare. 'Go into your study, Dadda,' I said, 'and bolt the door. Please.'

He nodded bemusedly and straightened up, holding on to my arm for support. 'Thanks, old boy,' he whispered and made a grotesque attempt to grin. 'That was a close call, wasn't it?'

I waited till the study door had shut behind him and I had heard the lock click. Then I returned to Betty. She was still lying where I had left her. I now saw, to my astonishment, that she was weeping. 'Come on, Ma,' I said. 'Get up.'

She looked up at me as though she were seeing me for the first time. 'You hurt me,' she whimpered in a voice so childish and so unlikely that I could scarcely believe my ears. 'You had no right to do that to your mother.'

'You leave him alone,' I said. 'That's all. Just *let him be*!'

'You hurt me,' she repeated. 'You don't know your own strength.'

'Come on. Get up.' I helped her to her feet and drew her into the drawing-room.

She held out her left arm for my inspection. Sure enough the marks of my fingers were clearly visible. 'I'm sorry,' I said. 'But it's your own fault.'

She stroked the bruise and sniffed wetly. 'He makes me so bloody mad, Col. Do you know what the bugger said to me?'

'No,' I said. 'And I don't *want* to know. I've heard too much already. But if you *touch* him again . . .'

She looked me up and down and then she laughed. 'Well, *you're* no pissy pacifist, that's for sure.'

I went out, closing the door behind me, and suddenly all my bravado drained away. I trembled from head to toe and my guts seemed to have turned to water. If the drawing-room door had opened at that moment I really don't know what I should have done.

That evening, after supper, I went in to see my father. His record of our interview has survived in his journal though the events which immediately preceded it have been excised. He described it thus: "Col went back to school this morning. He was very, very sweet to me yesterday evening. He is shy; but there is a depth of precious affection in him which did me good. Though it really hasn't been my fault, I feel guilty for having been so poor a father to Weg and Col. Engaged all the while in fighting for my own life, I have done little or nothing for either of them. The difference between the life with my children that I dreamed of before they were born and the reality is a masterpiece of irony. To think of the little pictures Katherine drew in the margin of one of her letters of 'our children', and then to think of the last ten years! And yet, in spite of all, my children are 'our children'—amazingly, uncannily so. Weg and Col; Mary and David—it's true of both the pairs. And I know Weg and Col understand, and have no grievance against me for my failure. On the contrary, Col made me feel that he loved me only the more for it."

What strikes *me* as supremely ironic about that entry is that in it Weg and I appear as Katherine's children and not as Violet's! Also my father has omitted to record that I pleaded with him to leave Larling for good. But, this apart, I'm sure it is a faithful account of the essence of our meeting. I knew

I had to make it clear to him that I trusted him and, as he well knew, 'trust' in that sense was but another word for love. In truth my heart ached for him. He seemed so frail, so utterly wretched, that it was almost as if our rôles were reversed. I cherished him as one day I would cherish my own children at times when the world seemed to have turned its back on them. Perhaps it did do him some good. I would like to think so.

31

I HAD been back at Rendcomb for little more than three weeks when I received a letter from my father telling me that he had left Betty and Larling for ever. 'I can see now,' he wrote, 'that I should have done it long ago; but what is crystal clear to me today wasn't at all clear then. Anyway I've crossed the Rubicon and burnt my boats into the bargain. It feels rather strange on this side of the water but I daresay I'll get used to it eventually.'

'This side of the water' was, for the time being at any rate, his room next to the *Peace News* offices in Finsbury Park and it was there that I wrote to him and told him that I was quite sure he had done the right thing. I added that I was resitting my 'Matric' in November and that the general opinion among the staff seemed to be that I was unlucky not to have got it in July.

News from Larling reached me in irregular dribbles. Rue wrote that she had been into Norwich for an interview with the N.A.A.F.I. and was hoping they would take her on as a cook. Since she would have had to stand on top of a box to see over a N.A.A.F.I. counter this seemed the best possible compromise if ever she was to get herself into uniform. I found I was quite incapable of imagining what the Old Rectory would be like without her.

Then Betty wrote to say that I was not to come home for the Christmas holidays. I had hardly digested this directive before a second letter arrived from her saying I *was* to come home and that Mary and David were counting on it. I decided to ignore the first letter and wrote back to Mary that I was looking forward to seeing her and David again and that I hoped we would have some snow.

When I got home in December Rue had already left and Betty—much to her chagrin—was having to accustom herself to life without domestic help. Her first question to me was had I seen 'that bitch' on my way through London? I assured her I hadn't. Had I seen *him*? There too I was guiltless. Having thus passed my examination at the frontier I was permitted to enter.

Mary and David were overjoyed to see me. I soon had Mary organized helping me to construct a primitive 'Kipp's' apparatus for the production of hydrogen. I obtained the dilute sulphuric acid necessary by baling a little out of each accumulator cell in the battery house and I used the gas I manufactured to fill toy balloons. Since my father would never have allowed me to tamper with the accumulators I chalked this up as the first positive advantage of his absence. The second was the marked relaxation of tension.

I discussed this with Weg one evening when we were both sitting beside the drawing-room fire after Betty had retired to bed. She agreed that things had been much better since my father had left. 'Hasn't she been on at you then?' I asked.

Weg shrugged. 'She made me write to him and beg him to come back.'

'Crikey!' I exclaimed. 'And did you?'

She just looked at me.

I nodded: it had been a stupid question. 'What's going to happen, d'you think?'

'I don't know,' she said.

'Will you stay here?'

She stared into the flames, seeing, no doubt, a host of grisly horrors that I could barely begin to imagine. With Rue gone only her love for Mary and young Dave remained to tether her to Larling. But her deepest loyalty had always been to my father. He was her God whom she adored with an unquestioning love far surpassing that of ordinary mortals. If he needed her either to stay or to go that would she do. Now she was a weekly boarder at Thretford, living in private lodgings, and was beginning to taste for the first time since that year in Belgium something of the almost forgotten delights of a normal life free from the tyranny of Betty. I was convinced, even as I looked at her, that it could be only a matter of time before she cut herself loose completely. I said as much. But she only repeated dreamily: 'I don't know, Col. I just don't know.'

I soon became aware that Betty's attitude towards me had changed remarkably. She must have reminded me at least a dozen times of how I had manhandled her in the summer. She had apparently displayed her bruises all around the neighbourhood like war medals. It gradually dawned on me that, in some weird way, she was actually *proud* of me for having done it, whereas I felt sick every time I remembered it.

That apart I enjoyed that holiday immensely. The snow came early in January. I constructed a toboggan, sat David on it and towed him round the lawn behind my bike. Every time I cornered he rolled off, shrieking with laughter, until in the end, encrusted with snow, he resembled a small, plump polar bear. Soon after came a series of heavy frosts and I took him and Mary sliding down on the frozen fens. The ice was still perilously thin and, more than once, it emitted a shrill and mysterious *wheep!* as we ventured out but, luckily, it held.

When the news came that I had passed my 'Matric' I went off skating by myself in lonely celebration. I must have gone for miles because the sun was setting as I turned for home. I felt ecstatically happy. Desolate and unbelievably beautiful, this misty frozen world was mine alone: I shared it with no one. As I sped back across the flaming ice, seemingly into the very eye of the sun, I burst out into a wild, spontaneous carol of pure joy.

Betty brought Mary and David down to the station to see me off. I kissed them both and told them that I'd write to them.

'We'll get the canoe going when I get back in April,' I said. 'It'll need painting up though. You can help me.'

The whistle shrilled. I leant out of the window and waved to them. They grew smaller and smaller as the train gathered speed. But they still stood there, hand in hand, two tiny little dots of affection, waving and waving after me.

32

IN the Lower 6th I finally came into my own. In three short weeks I had made up the work I had missed through having to re-sit my 'Matric'. When J. C. James handed back my first Higher Level European History essay on 'The Leaders of the Reformation' I saw that he had underlined certain passages in red ink and had scribbled in the margin '*Source?*' Since there was no source other than my own head I was as flattered as he was surprised.

During the term there were three full-scale stage productions all of which I was involved in—*Twelfth Night*, Marlowe's *Dr. Faustus*, and the melodrama *Sweeny Todd*. I had quite a large part in this last, and when my father wrote that he hoped to come down and see the production I was naturally delighted. Then, three days before he was due to arrive, I went down with mumps. Lee-Browne, who was producing the play, was convinced that I had contracted the disease because I was afraid of acting in front of my father. I understood his exasperation but pointed out that, in one way or another, I had been performing before my father all my life and that few things gave me more pleasure. He seemed to prefer his own explanation.

When my father arrived I was in bed with a giddy temperature, aching testicles, and a face like a cantaloup. In these circumstances it is perhaps understandable that I found some difficulty in concentrating upon what he was saying. He seemed to spend much of the time talking about a farm he was hoping to buy. Or was it about the Adelphi Centre which now had a small farming community attached to it? Somewhere between the two I got hopelessly confused and was relieved when, as he took his farewell, he told me he would be writing to me about it.

I went straight out of mumps into yellow jaundice—a progress that is not uncommon but is extremely unaesthetic. The features that now leered back at me out of the mirror might have belonged to some oriental *roué*, and my urine looked like Guinness. I almost began to wonder whether someone hadn't put a curse on me.

If they had they removed it before the end of term. I returned into circulation just in time to help clear the decks for the Easter holidays. The very morning I emerged from Sick Bay the letter which my father had promised me duly arrived. As I read it I experienced first astonishment, then bewilderment, and, finally, profound dismay. The gist of it was that I was not, after all, to return to Larling for my holiday but was to join him and Weg at Langham where he and the woman he was in love with had purchased a house. I now recalled his telling me that Weg had left Larling 'of her own free will' and had spent her half-term holiday with him. Since I had been expecting something of the kind I had simply accepted it at the time—had, indeed, expressed my warm approval. Could he have interpreted *that* as an indication that I wished to do the same?

I read the letter through again. Almost everything in it (it was mainly a retrospective review of his disastrous marriage with Betty) I agreed with absolutely. All but one thing. I did *not* want to leave Larling and Mary and David. But he seemed to be assuming that I *did*, that what I had so often said was right for *him* was therefore right for me too. There was no question about it. He simply took it for granted that I must wish to do what Weg had done. He even said he was 'counting on me to back him up'.

I racked my brain in an effort to recall anything I had said while he was sitting at my bedside that could have given him grounds for asking this of me. I could think of nothing at all. In fact, to the best of my recollection, I had gone out of my way to stress how dear Mary and David were to me. So how *could* he ask it? Why, it was barely a week since I had written to Mary telling her how much I was looking forward to seeing her again! And, God knows, it wasn't as if he *needed* me with him! He had Weg and the woman he loved, surely they were enough. Yet here he was appealing to *my* loyalty to him. It was unfair—monstrously unfair. Why, he wasn't thinking of *me* at all, but of *himself*, of *his* happiness!

In leaping to that conclusion, I was undoubtedly being less than fair to him, but not, I think, wholly unjust. In his journal entry covering his trip down to Rendcomb to see me he asks rhetorically: "Have I done right or wrong? A question to which there is no answer—in those terms. I have done what, in the deepest sense, I *had* to do." It is a wry and mocking imp that pops up to remind me that 'in the deepest sense' at an earlier time he had felt he *had* to marry Betty.

But his decision had impaled me on the horns of an intolerable dilemma. If I defied him and went back to Larling against his express wish, then not only would I forfeit his love, but would run the very real risk that sooner or later Betty would lose her temper with me and throw me out of the house. Where would I be then? If, on the other hand, I now joined him at Langham I would be damned as a traitor in Betty's eyes and would forfeit all chance of ever living at Larling again. I remembered Mary and David waving to me from the deserted platform and I felt misery like a clenched fist in my throat. For one awful moment I seemed to see Larling like something viewed down the wrong end of a telescope, wholly precious, infinitely diminished. And it was rushing away from me.

I walked out into the park and sat down on the brink of the precipitous slope overlooking the lake. Rooks were swirling among the tree tops below me. I took out his letter and read it through for the last time. Then, very deliberately, I tore it up into tiny shreds and let the breeze scatter them like snowflakes out over the abyss.

33

AND so it was that I too crossed my father's Rubicon and joined him on the far bank. But many years were to pass before I could drag myself away from the water's edge. For months I was to be haunted by a vision of Mary waiting for me in that echoing house. 'Why isn't Col here, Mummy? He *said* he was coming. When *is* he coming?' And the one person in the world I could not speak to about it was my father himself. I just knew it would be no use. Thirty years later I find my instinct confirmed by the conclusion of an entry in his journal made in April 1942, where, after lamenting the lack of any true "contact" between us, he says: "I suppose it's no *use* worrying. Yet I do. And I blame myself: yet I don't see what I am to blame myself *for*. In the case of Weg it was clear enough. *Ablata causa, tollitur effectus*. But in Col's case I don't understand the cause." Such gulfs are not bridgeable by words alone.

As he had arranged in that final letter he came to meet me at Paddington station. I don't think he was in the least surprised to see me. He told me that I was looking better than when he had seen me last. I have forgotten what I said in reply but it can hardly have been any indication of my true feelings.

We had lunch together and then he accompanied me to Liverpool Street. The Colchester train was already in. I climbed aboard and heaved my suitcase up on to the luggage rack. On the platform my father fidgeted from one foot to the other. I smiled down on him. 'Don't you bother to wait,' I told him. 'I'll be perfectly all right.'

'I suppose it must seem a bit of a plunge into the unknown, old boy.'

'Oh, I don't know,' I said. 'Frank's at Langham, isn't he?'

'Yes, he's there.'

'I haven't seen him for ages.'

'No, I don't suppose you have.'

There was an uncomfortable silence. 'Look,' I said. 'Don't *worry*. Really. I mean it.'

He reached up, grasped one of my hands in both of his, and

then he winked—one of those huge, devastatingly conspiratorial winks that only he could do. 'We'll meet on Wednesday, then.'

'Yes,' I said. 'But I shouldn't hang around now. You'll only catch cold.'

He nodded and turned away towards the station exit. As I watched him go I heard the station announcer broadcast that the 3.25 train for Cambridge, Ely and Norwich was about to depart. It was the one I would have been on had I been going back to Larling. I pulled at the leather strap which closed up the window and, not for the first time, found myself wondering about the woman who would be meeting me at Colchester. Suddenly, for no reason at all, a single phrase detached itself from the past and was there dancing around in my head. I remembered my father using it when I was trying to console him after that final terrible row. '*Forward over graves.*'

Like the last piece of a jig-saw puzzle it dropped into place. I now knew what it meant.